The Brother Lawrence Collection

The Brother Lawrence Collection
Practice and Presence of God
Spiritual Maxims
The Life of Brother Lawrence

by Brother Lawrence

©2008 Wilder Publications

Wilder Publications, LLC.
PO Box 3005
Radford VA 24143-3005

ISBN 10: 1-60459-251-6
ISBN 13: 978-1-60459-251-1

Practice and Presence of God
Book 1:

Preface 7
First Conversation 8
Second Conversation 10
Third Conversation 14
Fourth Conversation 16
First Letter 20
Second Letter 22
Third Letter 26
Fourth Letter 27
Fifth Letter 29
Sixth Letter 31
Seventh Letter 33
Eighth Letter 34
Ninth Letter 35
Tenth Letter 37
Eleventh Letter 38
Twelfth Letter 40
Thirteenth Letter 41
Fourteenth Letter 42
Fifteenth Letter 43
Notes 44

Preface

This book consists of notes of several conversations had with, and letters written by Nicholas Herman, of Lorraine, a lowly and unlearned man, who, after having been a footman and soldier, was admitted a Lay Brother among the bare-footed Carmelites at Paris in 1666, and was afterwards known as "Brother Lawrence."

His conversion, which took place when he was about eighteen years old, was the result, under God, of the mere sight in midwinter, of a dry and leafless tree, and of the reflections it stirred respecting the change the coming spring would bring. From that time he grew eminently in the knowledge and love of GOD, endeavoring constantly to walk *as in His presence.* No wilderness wanderings seem to have intervened between the Red Sea and the Jordan of his experience. A wholly consecrated man, he lived his Christian life through as a pilgrim—as a steward and not as an owner, and died at the age of eighty, leaving a name which has been as "ointment poured forth."

The "Conversations" are supposed to have been written by M. Beaufort, Grand Vicar to M. de Chalons, formerly Cardinal de Noailles, by whose recommendation the letters were first published.

The book has, within a short time, gone through repeated English and American editions, and has been a means of blessing to many souls. It contains very much of that wisdom which only lips the Lord has touched can express, and which only hearts He has made teachable can receive.

May this edition also be blessed by GOD, and redound to the praise of the glory of His grace.

First Conversation

The first time I saw *Brother Lawrence*, was upon the 3d of August, 1666. He told me that GOD had done him a singular favor, in his conversion at the age of eighteen.

That in the winter, seeing a tree stripped of its leaves, and considering that within a little time the leaves would be renewed and after that the flowers and fruit appear, he received a high view of the Providence and Power of GOD, which has never since been effaced from his soul. That this view had perfectly set him loose from the world, and kindled in him such a love for GOD, that he could not tell whether it had increased during the more than forty years he had lived since.

That he had been footman to M. Fieubert, the treasurer, and that he was a great awkward fellow who broke everything.

That he had desired to be received into a monastery, thinking that he would there be made to smart for his awkwardness and the faults he should commit, and so he should sacrifice to GOD his life, with its pleasures: but that God had disappointed him, he having met with nothing but satisfaction in that state.

That we should establish ourselves in a sense of GOD'S Presence, by continually conversing with Him. That it was a shameful thing to quit His conversation, to think of trifles and fooleries.

That we should feed and nourish our souls with high notions of GOD; which would yield us great joy in being devoted to Him.

That we ought to *quicken*, i.e., *to enliven, our faith*. That it was lamentable we had so little; and that instead of taking *faith* for the rule of their conduct, men amused themselves with trivial devotions, which changed daily. That the way of

Faith was the spirit of the Church, and that it was sufficient to bring us to a high degree of perfection.

That we ought to give ourselves up to GOD, with regard both to things temporal and spiritual, and seek our satisfaction only in the fulfilling of His will, whether he lead us by suffering or by consolation, for all would lie equal to a soul truly resigned. That there needed fidelity in those dryness, or insensibilities and irksomenesses in prayer, by which GOD tries our love to him; that *then* was the time for us to make good and effectual acts of resignation, whereof one alone would oftentimes very much promote our spiritual advancement.

That as for the miseries and sins he heard of daily in the world, he was so far from wondering at them, that, on the contrary, he was surprised that there were not more, considering the malice sinners were capable of; that for his part he prayed for them; but knowing that GOD could remedy the mischiefs they did when He pleased, he gave himself no farther trouble.

That to arrive at such resignation as GOD requires, we should watch attentively over all the passions which mingle as well in spiritual things as in those of a grosser nature; that GOD would give light concerning those passions to those who truly desire to serve Him. That if this was my design, viz., sincerely to serve GOD, I might come to him (B. Lawrence) as often as I pleased, without any Fear of being troublesome; but if not, that I ought no more to visit him.

Second Conversation

That he had always been governed by love, without selfish views; and that having resolved to make the love of GOD the *end* of all his actions, he had found reasons to be well satisfied with his method. That he was pleased when he could take up a straw from the ground for the love of GOD, seeking Him only, and nothing else, not even His gifts.

That he had been long troubled in mind from a certain belief that he should be damned; that all the men in the world could not have persuaded him to the contrary; but that he had thus reasoned with himself about it: *I engaged in a religious life only for the love of GOD, and I have endeavored to act only for Him; whatever becomes of me, whether I be lost or saved, I will always continue to act purely for the love of GOD. I shall have this good at least, that till death I shall have done all that is in me to love Him.* That this trouble of mind had lasted four years; during which time he had suffered much. But that at last he had seen that this trouble arose from want of faith; and that since then he had passed his life in perfect liberty and continual joy. That he had placed his sins betwixt him and GOD, as it were, to tell Him that he did not deserve His favors, but that GOD still continued to bestow them in abundance.

That in order to form a habit of conversing with GOD continually, and referring all we do to Him, we must at first apply to Him with some diligence: but that after a little care we should find His love inwardly excite us to it without any difficulty.

That he expected after the pleasant days GOD had given him, he should have his turn of pain and suffering; but that he was not uneasy about it, knowing very well, that as he could do nothing of himself, GOD would not fail to give him the strength to bear it.

That when an occasion of practicing some virtue offered, he addressed himself to GOD, saying, LORD, *I cannot do this unless Thou enablest me*: and that then he received strength more than sufficient.

That when he had failed in his duty, he only confessed his fault, saying to GOD, *I shall never do otherwise, if You leave me to myself; it is You who must hinder my falling, and mend what is amiss*. That after this, he gave himself no further uneasiness about it.

That we ought to act with GOD in the greatest simplicity, speaking to Him frankly and plainly, and imploring His assistance in our affairs, just as they happen. That GOD never failed to grant it, as he had often experienced.

That he had been lately sent into Burgundy, to buy the provision of wine for the society, which was a very unwelcome task for him, because he had no turn for business, and because he was lame and could not go about the boat but by rolling himself over the casks. That however he gave himself no uneasiness about it, nor about the purchase of the wine. That he said to GOD, *It was His business he was about*, and that he afterwards found it very well performed. That he had been sent into Auvergne, the year before, upon the same account; that he could not tell how the matter passed, but that it proved very well.

So, likewise, in his business in the kitchen (to which he had naturally a great aversion), having accustomed himself to do everything there for the love of GOD, and with prayer, upon all occasions, for His grace to do his work well, he had found everything easy, during fifteen years that he had been employed there.

That he was very well pleased with the post he was now in; but that he was as ready to quit that as the former, since he was always pleasing himself in every condition, by doing little things for the love of GOD.

That with him the set times of prayer were not different from other times; that he retired to pray, according to the directions of his Superior, but that he did not want such retirement, nor ask for it, because his greatest business did not divert him from GOD.

That as he knew his obligation to love GOD in all things, and as he endeavored so to do, he had no need of a director to advise him, but that he needed much a Confessor to absolve him. That he was very sensible of his faults, but not discouraged by them; that he confessed them to GOD, but did not plead against Him to excuse them. When he had so done, he peaceably resumed his usual practice of love and adoration.

That in his trouble of mind, he had consulted nobody, but knowing only by the light of faith that GOD was present, he contented himself with directing all his actions to Him, *i.e.*, doing them with a desire to please Him, let what would come of it.

That useless thoughts spoil all: that the mischief began there; but that we ought to reject them, as soon as we perceived their impertinence to the matter in hand, or our salvation; and return to our communion with GOD.

That at the beginning he had often passed his time appointed for prayer, in rejecting wandering thoughts, and falling back into them. That he could never regulate his devotion by certain methods as some do. That nevertheless, at first he had *meditated* for some time, but afterwards that went off, in a manner he could give no account of.

That all bodily mortifications and other exercises are useless, except as they serve to arrive at the union with GOD by love; that he had well considered this, and found it the shortest way to go straight to Him by a continual exercise of love, and doing all things for His sake.

That we ought to make a great difference between the acts of the *understanding* and those of the *will*: that the first were comparatively of little value, and the others, all. That our only business was to love and delight ourselves in GOD.

That all possible kinds of mortification, if they were void of the love of GOD, could not efface a single sin. That we ought, without anxiety, to expect the pardon of our sins from the Blood of JESUS CHRIST, only endeavoring to love Him with all our hearts. That GOD seemed to have granted the greatest favors to the greatest sinners, as more signal monuments of his mercy.

That the greatest pains or pleasures of this world, were not to be compared with what he had experienced of both kinds in a spiritual state: so that he was careful for nothing and feared nothing, desiring only one thing of GOD, viz., that he might not offend Him.

That he had no scruples; for, said he, when I *fail* in my duty, I readily acknowledge it, saying, *I am used to do so: I shall never do otherwise, if I am left to myself.* I fail not, then I give GOD thanks, acknowledging the strength comes from Him.

Third Conversation

He told me that the *foundation of the spiritual life* in *him*, had been a high notion and esteem of GOD in faith; which when he had once well conceived, he had no other care at first, but faithfully to reject every other thought, *that he might perform all his actions for the love of* GOD. That when sometimes he had not thought of GOD for a good while, he did not disquiet himself for it; but after having acknowledged his wretchedness to GOD, he returned to Him with so much the greater trust in Him, as he had found himself wretched through forgetting Him.

That the trust we put in GOD, honors Him much, and draws down great graces.

That it was impossible, not only that GOD should deceive, hut also that He should long let a soul suffer which is perfectly resigned to Him, and resolved to endure everything for His sake.

That he had so often experienced the ready succors of Divine Grace upon all occasions, that from the same experience, when he had business to do, he did not think of it beforehand; but when it was time to do it, he found in GOD, as in a clear mirror, all that was fit for him to do. That of late he had acted thus, without anticipating care; but before the experience above mentioned, he had used it in his affairs.

When outward business diverted him a little from the thought of GOD, a fresh remembrance coming from GOD invested his soul, and so inflamed and transported him that it was difficult for him to contain himself.

That he was more united to GOD in his outward employments, than when he left them for devotion in retirement.

That he expected hereafter some great pain of body or mind; that the worst that could happen to him was, to lose that sense of GOD which he had enjoyed so long; but that the goodness of GOD assured him He would not forsake him utterly, and that He would give him strength to bear whatever evil He permitted to happen to him; and therefore that he feared nothing, and had no occasion to consult with anybody about his state. That when he had attempted to do it, he had always come away more perplexed; and that as he was conscious of his readiness to lay down his life for the love of GOD, he had no apprehension of danger. That perfect resignation to GOD was a sure way to heaven, a way in which we had always sufficient light for our conduct.

That in the beginning of the spiritual life, we ought to be faithful in doing our duty and denying ourselves; but after that, unspeakable pleasures followed; that in difficulties we need only have recourse to JESUS CHRIST, and beg his grace; with that everything became easy.

That many do not advance in the Christian progress because they stick in penances, and particular exercises, while they neglect the love of GOD, which is the *end*. That this appeared plainly by their works, and was the *reason* why we see so little solid virtue.

That there needed neither art nor science for going to GOD, but only a heart resolutely determined to apply itself to nothing but Him, or for *His* sake, and to love him only.

Fourth Conversation

He discoursed with me very frequently, and with great openness of heart concerning his manner of *going* to GOD, whereof some part is related already.

He told me that all consists *in one hearty renunciation* of everything which we are sensible does not lead to GOD; that we might accustom ourselves to a continual conversation with Him, with freedom and in simplicity. That we need only to recognize GOD intimately present with us, to address ourselves to Him every moment, that we may beg His assistance for knowing His will in things doubtful, and for rightly performing those which we plainly see he requires of us, offering them to Him before we do them, and giving Him thanks when we have done.

That in this conversation with God, we are also employed in praising, adoring and loving Him incessantly, for His infinite goodness and perfection.

That, without being discouraged on account of our sins, we should pray for His grace with a perfect confidence, as relying upon the infinite merits of our LORD JESUS CHRIST. That GOD never failed offering us His grace at each action; that he distinctly perceived it, and never failed of it, unless when his thoughts had wandered from a sense of GOD'S Presence, or he had forgotten to ask His assistance.

That GOD always gave us light in our doubts, when we had no other design but ask to please Him.

That our sanctification did not depend upon *changing* our works, but in doing that for GOD's sake, which we commonly do for our own. That it was lamentable to see how many people mistook the means for the end, addicting themselves to certain works, which they performed very imperfectly, by reason of their human or selfish regards.

That the most excellent method he had found of going to GOD, was that of doing our common business without any view of pleasing men,[1] and (as far as we are capable) purely for the love of GOD.

That it was a great delusion to think that the times of prayer ought to differ from other times: that we are as strictly obliged to adhere to GOD by action in the time of action, as by prayer in the season of prayer.

That his prayer was nothing else but a sense of the presence of GOD, his soul being at that time insensible to everything but Divine love: and that when the appointed times of prayer were past, he found no difference, because he still continued with GOD, praising and blessing Him with all his might, so that he passed his life in continual joy; yet hoped that GOD would give him somewhat to suffer, when he should grow stronger.

That we ought, once for all, heartily to put our whole trust in GOD, and make a total surrender of ourselves to Him, secure that He would not deceive us.

That we ought not to be weary of doing little things for the love of GOD, who regards not the greatness of the work, but the love with which it is performed. That we should not wonder if, in the beginning, we often failed in our endeavors, but that at last we should gain a habit, which will naturally produce its acts in us, without our care, and to our exceeding great delight.

That the whole substance of religion was faith, hope and charity; by the practice of which we become united to the will of GOD: that all besides is indifferent, and to be used as a means that we may arrive at our end, and be swallowed up therein, by faith and charity.

That all things are possible to him who *believes*—that they are less difficult to him who *hopes*—that they are more easy to him who *loves*, and still more easy to him who perseveres in the practice of these three virtues.

That the end we ought to propose to ourselves is to become, in this life, the most perfect worshippers of GOD we can possibly be, as we hope to be through all eternity.

That when we enter upon the spiritual life, we should consider, and examine to the bottom, what we are. And then we should find ourselves worthy of all contempt, and not deserving indeed the name of Christians: subject to all kinds of misery and numberless accidents, which trouble us and cause perpetual vicissitudes in our health, in our humors, in our internal and external dispositions; in fine, persons whom GOD would humble by many pains and labors, as well within as without. After this we should not wonder that troubles, temptations, oppositions and contradictions happen to us from men. We ought, on the contrary, to submit ourselves to them, and bear them as long as GOD pleases, as things highly advantageous to us.

That the greater perfection a soul aspires after, the more dependent it is upon Divine grace.

[2]Being questioned by one of his own society (to whom he was obliged to open himself) by what means he had attained such an habitual sense of GOD, he told him that, since his first coming to the monastery, he had considered GOD as the end of all his thoughts and desires, as the mark to which they should tend, and in which they should terminate.

That in the beginning of his noviciate, he spent the hours appointed for private prayer in thinking of GOD, so as to convince his mind of, and to impress deeply upon his heart, the Divine existence, rather by devout sentiments, and submission to the lights of faith, than by studied reasonings and elaborate meditations. That by this short and sure method, he exercised himself in the knowledge and love of GOD, resolving to use his utmost endeavor to live, in a continual sense of His Presence, and if possible, never to forget Him more.

That when he had thus in prayer filled his mind with great sentiments of that infinite Being, he went to his work appointed in the kitchen (for he was cook to the society); there having first considered severally the things his office required, and when and how each thing was to be done, he spent all the intervals of his time, as well before as after his work, in prayer.

That when he began his business, he said to GOD, with a filial trust in Him, "O my GOD, since Thou art with me, and I must now, in obedience to Thy commands, apply my mind to these outward things, I beseech Thee to grant me the grace to continue in Thy Presence; and to this end do Thou prosper me with Thy assistance, receive all my works, and possess all my affections."

As he proceeded in his work, he continued his familiar conversation with his Maker,—imploring His grace, and offering to Him all his actions.

When he had finished, he examined himself how he had discharged his duty; if he found *well*, he returned thanks to GOD; if otherwise, he asked pardon; and without being discouraged, he set his mind right again, and continued his exercise of the *presence* of GOD, as if he had never deviated from it. "Thus," said he, "by rising after my falls, and by frequently renewed acts of faith and love, I am come to a state wherein it would be as difficult for me not to think of GOD as it was at first to accustom myself to it."

As brother Lawrence had found such an advantage in walking in the presence of GOD, it was natural for him to recommend it earnestly to others; but his example was a stronger inducement than any arguments he could propose. His very countenance was edifying, such a sweet and calm devotion appearing in it as could not but effect the beholders. And it was observed that in the greatest hurry of business in the kitchen, he still preserved his recollection and heavenly-mindedness. He was never hasty nor loitering, but did each thing in its season, with an even, uninterrupted composure and tranquility of spirit. "The time of business," said he, "does not with me differ from the time of prayer; and in the noise and clatter of my kitchen, while several persons are at the same time calling for different things, I possess GOD in as great tranquility as if I were upon my knees at the blessed sacrament."

First Letter

Since you desire so earnestly that I should communicate to you the method by which I arrived at that *habitual sense of GOD'S Presence*, which our LORD, of His mercy, has been pleased to vouch-safe to me, I must tell you that it is with great difficulty that I am prevailed on by your importunities; and now I do it only upon the terms that you show my letter to nobody. If I knew that you should let it be seen, all the desire that I have for your advancement would not be able to determine me to it. The account I can give you is:

Having found in many books different methods of going to GOD, and divers practices of the spiritual life, I thought this would serve rather to puzzle me than facilitate what I sought after, which was nothing but how to become wholly GOD'S. This made me resolve to give the all for the all; so after having given myself wholly to GOD, that He might take away my sin, *I renounced, for the love of Him, everything that was not He; and I began to live as if there was none but He and I in the world.* Sometimes I considered myself before Him as a poor criminal at the feet of his judge; at other times I beheld Him in my heart as my FATHER, as my GOD: I worshipped Him the oftenest that I could, keeping my mind in His holy Presence, and recalling it as often as I found it wandered from Him. I found no small pain in this exercise, and yet I continued it, notwithstanding all the difficulties that occurred, without troubling or disquieting myself when my mind had wandered involuntarily. I made this my business as much all the day long as at the appointed times of prayer; for at all times, every hour, every minute, even in the height of my business, I drove away from my mind everything that was capable of interrupting my thought of GOD.

Such has been my common practice ever since I entered in religion; and, though I have done it very imperfectly, yet I have found great advantages by it. These, I well know, are to be imputed to the mere mercy and goodness of GOD, because we can do nothing without Him; and *I* still less than any. But when we are faithful to keep ourselves in His holy Presence, and set Him always before us, this not only hinders our offending Him, and doing anything that may displease Him, at least wilfully, but it also begets in us a holy freedom, and, if I may so speak, a familiarity with GOD, wherewith we ask, and that successfully, the graces we stand in need of. In fine, by often repeating these acts, they become *habitual*, and the presence of GOD rendered as it were *natural to* us Give Him thanks, if you please, with me, for His great goodness towards me, which I can never sufficiently admire, for the many favors He has done to so miserable a sinner as I am. May all things praise Him. Amen.

I am, in our LORD, yours, etc.

Second Letter

To the Reverend ____

Not finding my manner of life in books, although I have no difficulty about it, yet, for greater security, I shall be glad to know your thoughts concerning it.

In a conversation some days since with a person of piety, he told me the spiritual life was a life of grace, which begins with servile fear, which is increased by hope of eternal life, and which is consummated by pure love. That each of these states had its different stages, by which one arrives at last at that blessed consummation.

I have not followed all these methods. On the contrary, from I know not what instincts, I found they discouraged me. This was the reason why, at my entrance into religion, I took a resolution to give myself up to GOD, as the best return I could make for His love; and, for the love of Him, to renounce all besides.

For the first year I commonly employed myself during the time set apart for devotion with the thought of death, judgment, heaven, hell, and my sins, Thus continued some years, applying my mind carefully the rest of the day, and even in the midst of my business, *to the presence of* GOD, whom I considered always as *with* me, often as *in* me.

At length I came insensibly to do the same thing during my set time of prayer, which caused in me great delight and consolation. This practice produced in me so high an esteem for GOD, that *faith* alone was capable to satisfy me in that point.[3]

Such was my beginning; and yet I must tell you that for the first ten years I suffered much: the apprehension that I was not devoted to GOD as I wished to be, my past sins always present to my mind, and the great unmerited favors which GOD did me, were the matter and source of my sufferings.

During this time I fell often, and rose again presently. It seemed to me that all creatures, reason, and GOD Himself were against me; and *faith* alone for me. I was troubled sometimes with thoughts that to believe I had received such favors was an effect of my presumption, which pretended to be *at once* where others arrive with difficulty; at other times that it was a wilful delusion, and that there was no salvation for me.

When I thought of nothing but to end my days in these troubles (which did not at all diminish the trust I had in GOD, and which served only to increase my faith), I found myself changed all at once; and my soul, which, till that time, was in trouble, felt a profound inward peace, as if she were in her centre and place of rest.

Ever since that time I walk before GOD simply, in faith, with humility and with love; and I apply myself diligently to do nothing and think nothing which may displease Him. I hope that when I have done what I can, He will do with me what He pleases.

As for what passes in me at present, I cannot express it. I have no pain or difficulty about my state, because I have no will but that of GOD, which I endeavor to accomplish in all things, and to which I am so resigned that I would not take up a straw from the ground against His order, or from any other motive than purely that of love to Him.

I have quitted all forms of devotion and set prayers but those to which my state obliges me. And I make it my business only to persevere in His holy presence, wherein I keep myself by a simple attention, and a general fond regard to GOD, which I may call an *actual presence of* GOD; or, to speak better, an habitual, silent and secret conversation of the soul with GOD, which often causes me joys and raptures inwardly, and sometimes also outwardly, so great, that I am forced to use means to moderate them and prevent their appearance to others.

In short, I am assured beyond all doubt that my soul has been with GOD above these thirty years. I pass over many things that I may not be tedious to you, yet I think it proper to inform you after what manner I consider myself before GOD, whom I behold as my King.

I consider myself as the most wretched of men, full of sores and corruption, and who has committed all sorts of crimes against his King; touched with a sensible regret, I confess to him all my wickedness, I ask His forgiveness, I abandon myself in His hands that He may do what he pleases with me. The King, full of mercy and goodness, very far from chastising me, embraces me with love, makes me eat at His table, serves me with His own hands, gives me the key of His treasures; He converses and delights Himself with me incessantly, in a thousand and a thousand ways, and treats me in all respects as His favorite. It is thus I consider myself from time to time in His holy presence.

My most useful method is this simple attention, and such a general passionate regard to GOD; to whom I find myself often attached with greater sweetness and delight than that of an infant at the mother's breast; so that, if I dare use the expression, I should choose to call this state the bosom, of GOD, for the inexpressible sweetness which I taste and experience there.

If sometimes my thoughts wander from it by necessity or infirmity, I am presently recalled by inward motions so charming and delicious that I am ashamed to mention them. I desire your reverence to reflect rather upon my great wretchedness, of which you are fully informed, than upon the great favors which GOD does me, all unworthy and ungrateful as I am.

As for my set hours of prayer, they are only a continuation of the same exercise. Sometimes I consider myself there as a stone before a carver, whereof he is to make a statue; presenting myself thus before GOD, I desire Him to form His perfect image in my soul, and make me entirely like Himself.

At other times, when I apply myself to prayer, I feel all my spirit and all my soul lift itself up without any care or effort of mine, and it continues as it were suspended and firmly fixed in GOD, as in its centre and place of rest.

I know that some charge this state with inactivity, delusion and self-love. I confess that it is a holy inactivity, and would be a happy self-love, if the soul in that state were capable of it; because, in effect, while she is in this repose, she cannot be disturbed by such acts as she was formerly accustomed to, and which were then her support, but which would now rather hinder than assist her.

Yet I cannot bear that this should be called delusion; because the soul which thus enjoys GOD desires herein nothing but Him. If this be delusion in me, it belongs to GOD to remedy it. Let Him do what He pleases with me; I desire only Him, and to be wholly devoted to Him. You will, however, oblige me in sending me your opinion, to which I always pay a great deference, for I have a singular esteem for your reverence, and am in our LORD,

Yours, etc.

Third Letter

We have a GOD who is infinitely gracious and knows all our wants. I always thought that He would reduce you to extremity. He will come in His own time, and when you least expect it. Hope in Him more than ever; thank Him with me for the favors he does you, particularly for the fortitude and patience which He gives you in your afflictions. It is a plain mark of the care He takes of you. Comfort yourself, then, with Him, and give thanks for all.

I admire also the fortitude and bravery of Mr. ____. God has given him a good disposition and a good will; but there is in him still a little of the world, and a great deal of youth. I hope the affliction which GOD has sent him will prove a wholesome remedy to him, and make him enter into himself. It is an accident which should engage him to put all his trust in *Him* who accompanies him everywhere. Let him think of Him as often as he can, especially in the greatest dangers. A little lifting up of the heart suffices. A little remembrance of GOD, one act of inward worship, though upon a march, and a sword in hand, are prayers, which, however short, are nevertheless very acceptable to GOD; and far from lessening a soldier's courage in occasions of danger, they best serve to fortify it.

Let him then think of GOD the most he can. Let him accustom himself, by degrees, to this small but holy exercise. No one will notice it, and nothing is easier than to repeat often in the day these little internal adorations. Recommend to him, if you please, that he think of GOD the most he can, in the manner here directed. It is very fit and most necessary for a soldier, who is daily exposed to the dangers of life. I hope that GOD will assist him and all the family, to whom I present my service, being theirs and Yours, etc.

Fourth Letter

I have taken this opportunity to communicate to you the sentiments of one of our society, concerning the admirable effects and continual assistances which he receives from *the presence of* GOD. Let you and me both profit by them.

You must know his continual care has been, for about forty years past that he has spent in religion, to be *always with* GOD, and to do nothing, say nothing, and think nothing which may displease Him; and this without any other view than purely for the love of Him, and because he deserves infinitely more.

He is now so accustomed to that *Divine Presence*, that he receives from it continual succors upon all occasions. For about thirty years, his soul has been filled with joys so continual, and sometimes so great, that he is forced to use means to moderate them, and to hinder their appearing outwardly.

If sometimes he is a little too much absent from that *Divine Presence*, GOD presently makes Himself to be felt in his soul to recall him, which often happens when he is most engaged in his outward business. He answers with exact fidelity to these inward drawings, either by an elevation of his heart towards GOD, or by a meek and fond regard to Him, or by such words as love forms upon these occasions, as for instance, *My God, here I am all devoted to Thee*: LORD, *make me according to Thy heart*. And then it seems to him (as in effect he feels it) that this GOD of love, satisfied with such few words, reposes again, and rests in the fund and centre of his soul. The experience of these things gives him such an assurance that GOD is always in the fund or bottom of his soul, that it renders him incapable of doubting it upon any account whatever.

Judge by this what content and satisfaction he enjoys while he continually finds in himself so great a treasure. He is no longer in an anxious search after it, but has it open before him, and may take what he pleases of it.

He complains much of our blindness, and cries often that we are to be pitied who content ourselves with so little. GOD, saith he, *has infinite treasure to bestow, and we take up with a little sensible devotion, which passes in a moment. Blind as we are, we hinder GOD, and stop the current of His graces. But when He finds a soul penetrated with a lively faith, He pours into it His graces and favors plentifully: there they flow like a torrent, which, after being forcibly stopped against its ordinary course, when it has found a passage, spreads itself with impetuosity and abundance.*

Yes, we often stop this torrent by the little value we set upon it. But let us stop it no more; let us enter into ourselves and break down the bank which hinders it. Let us make way for grace; let us redeem the lost time, for perhaps we have but little left. Death follows us close; let us be well prepared for it: for we die but once; and a miscarriage *there* is irretrievable.

I say again, let us enter into ourselves. The time presses, there is no room for delay: our souls are at stake. I believe you have taken such effectual measures that you will not be surprised. I commend you for it; it is the one thing necessary. We must, nevertheless, always work at it, because not to advance in the spiritual life is to go back. But those who have the gale of the HOLY SPIRIT go forward even in sleep. If the vessel of our soul is still tossed with winds and storms, let us awake the LORD, who reposes in it, and He will quickly calm the sea.

I have taken the liberty to impart to you these good sentiments, that you may compare them with your own. It will serve again to kindle and inflame them, if by misfortune (which GOD forbid, for it would be indeed a great misfortune) they should be, though never so little, cooled. Let us then *both* recall our first fervors. Let us profit by the example and the sentiments of this brother, who is little known of the world, but known of GOD, and extremely caressed by Him. I will pray for you; do you pray instantly for me, who am, in our LORD.

Yours, etc.

Fifth Letter

I received this day two books and a letter from Sister ____, who is preparing to make her profession, and upon that account desires the prayers of your holy society, and yours in particular. I perceive that she reckons much upon them; pray do not disappoint her. Beg of GOD that she may make her sacrifice in the view of His love alone, and with a firm resolution to be wholly devoted to Him. I will send you one of these books which treat of *the presence of* GOD; a subject which, in my opinion, contains the whole spiritual life; and it seems to me that whoever duly practices it will soon become spiritual.

I know that for the right practice of it, the heart must be empty of all other things; because GOD will possess the heart *alone*; and as He cannot possess it *alone* without emptying it of all besides, so neither can He act *there*, and do in it what He pleases, unless it be left vacant to Him.

There is not in the world a kind of life more sweet and delightful than that of a continual conversation with GOD. Those only can comprehend it who practice and experience it; yet I do not advise you to do it from that motive. It is not pleasure which we ought to seek in this exercise; but let us do it from a principle of love, and because GOD would have us.

Were I a preacher, I should, above all other things, preach the practice of *the presence of* GOD; and, were I a director, I should advise all the world to do it, so necessary do I think it, and so easy too.

Ah! knew we but the want we have of the grace and assistance of GOD, we should never lose sight of Him, no, not for a moment. Believe me; make immediately a holy and firm resolution never more wilfully to forget Him, and to spend the rest of your days in His sacred presence, deprived for the love of Him, if He thinks fit, of all consolations.

Set heartily about this work, and if you do it as you ought, be assured that you will soon find the effects of it. I will assist you with my prayers, poor as they are. I recommend myself earnestly to yours and those of your holy society being theirs, and more particularly

Yours, etc.

Sixth Letter

To the Same.

I have received from Mrs. ____, the things which you gave her for me. I wonder that you have not given me your thoughts of the little book I sent to you, and which you must have received. Pray set heartily about the practice of it in your old age: it is better late than never.

I cannot imagine how religious persons can live satisfied without the practice of *the presence of* GOD. For my part. I keep myself retired with Him in the fund or centre of my soul as much as I can; and while I am so with Him I fear nothing, but the least turning from Him is insupportable.

This exercise does not much fatigue the body; it is, however, proper to deprive it sometimes, nay often; of many little pleasures which are innocent and lawful, for GOD will not permit that a soul which desires to be devoted entirely to Him should take other pleasures than with Him: that is more than reasonable.

I do not say that therefore we must put any violent constraint upon ourselves. No, we must serve GOD in a holy freedom; we must do our business faithfully; without trouble or disquiet, recalling our mind to GOD mildly, and with tranquility, as often as we find it wandering from Him.

It is, however, necessary to put our whole trust in GOD, laying aside all other cares, and even some particular forms of devotion, though very good in themselves, yet such as one often engages in unreasonably, because these devotions are only means to attain to the end. So when by this exercise of *the presence of* GOD we are *with Him* who is our end, it is then useless to return to the means; but we may continue with Him our commerce of love, persevering in His holy presence, one while by an act of praise, of adoration or of desire; one while by an act of resignation or thanksgiving; and in all the ways which our spirit can invent.

Be not discouraged by the repugnance which you may find in it from nature; you must do yourself violence. At the first one often thinks it lost time, but you must go on, and resolve to persevere in it to death, notwithstanding all the difficulties that may occur. I recommend myself to the prayers of your holy society, and yours in particular. I am, in our LORD,

Yours, etc.

Seventh Letter

I pity you much. It will be of great importance if you can leave the care of your affairs to ____, and spend the remainder of your life only in worshiping GOD. He requires no great matters of us; a little remembrance of Him from time to time; a little adoration; sometimes to pray for His grace, sometimes to offer Him your sufferings, and sometimes to return Him thanks for the favors He has given you, and still gives you, in the midst of your troubles, and to console yourself with Him the oftenest you can. Lift up your heart to Him, sometimes even at your meals, and when you are in company: the least little remembrance will always be acceptable to Him. You need not cry very loud; He is nearer to us than we are aware of.

It is not necessary for being with GOD to be always at church: we may make an oratory of our heart wherein to retire from time to time to converse with Him in meekness, humility and love. Every one is capable of such familiar conversation with GOD, some more, some less: He knows what we can do. Let us begin, then. Perhaps He expects but one generous resolution on our part. Have courage. We have but little time to live; you are near sixty-four, and I am almost eighty. Let us live and die with GOD. Sufferings will be sweet and pleasant to us while we are with Him; and the greatest pleasures will be, without Him, a cruel punishment to us. May He be blessed for all. Amen.

Accustom yourself, then, by degrees thus to worship Him, to beg His grace, to offer Him your heart from time to time in the midst of your business, even every moment, if you can. Do not always scrupulously confine yourself to certain rules, or particular forms of devotion, but act with a general confidence in GOD, with love and humility. You may assure — of my poor prayers, and that I am their servant, and particularly

Yours in our LORD, etc.

Eighth Letter

(Concerning wandering thoughts in Prayer.)

You tell me nothing new; you are not the only one that is troubled with wandering thoughts. Our mind is extremely roving; but, as the will is mistress of all our faculties, she must recall them, and carry them to GOD as their last end.

When the mind, for want of being sufficiently reduced by recollection at our first engaging in devotion, has contracted certain bad habits of wandering and dissipation, they are difficult to overcome, and commonly draw us, even against our wills, to the things of the earth.

I believe one remedy for this is to confess our faults, and to humble ourselves before GOD. I do not advise you to use multiplicity of words in prayer: many words and long discourses being often the occasions of wandering. Hold yourself in prayer before GOD, like a dumb or paralytic beggar at a rich man's gate. Let it be *your* business to keep your mind in the presence of the LORD. If it sometimes wander and withdraw itself from Him, do not much disquiet yourself for that: trouble and disquiet serve rather to distract the mind than to re-collect it: the will must bring it back in tranquility. If you persevere in this manner, GOD will have pity on you.

One way to re-collect the mind easily in the time of prayer, and preserve it more in tranquility, is *not to let it wander too far at other times*: you should keep it strictly in the presence of GOD; and being accustomed to think of Him often, you will find it easy to keep your mind calm in the time of prayer, or at least to recall it from its wanderings.

I have told you already at large, in my former letters, of the advantages we may draw from this practice of the presence of GOD: let us set about it seriously, and pray for one another.

Yours, etc.

Ninth Letter

The enclosed is an answer to that which I received from ____; pray deliver it to her. She seems to me full of good will, but she would go faster than grace. One does not become holy all at once. I recommend her to you: we ought to help one another by our advice, and yet more by our good examples. You will oblige me to let me hear of her from time to time, and whether she be very fervent and very obedient.

Let us thus think often that our only business in this life is to please GOD, and that all besides is but folly and vanity. You and I have lived about forty years in religion (*i.e.*, a monastic life). Have we employed them in loving and serving GOD, who by His mercy has called us to this state and for that very end? I am filled with shame and confusion when I reflect on one hand upon the great favors which GOD has done, and incessantly continues to do me; and on the other, upon the ill use I have made of them, and my small advancement in the way of perfection.

Since by His mercy He gives us still a little time, let us begin in earnest: let us repair the lost time: let us return with a full assurance to that FATHER of mercies, who is always ready to receive us affectionately. Let us renounce, let us generously renounce, for the love of Him, all that is not Himself; He deserves infinitely more. Let us think of Him perpetually. Let us put all our trust in Him. I doubt not but we shall soon find the effects of it in receiving the abundance of His grace, with which we can do all things, and without which we can do nothing but sin.

We cannot escape the dangers which abound in life without the actual and *continual* help of GOD: let us then pray to Him for it *continually*. How can we pray to Him without being with Him? How can we be with Him but in thinking of Him often? And how can we often think of Him, but by a holy habit which we should form of it? You will tell me that I am always saying the same thing. It is true, for this is the best and easiest method I know; and as I use no other, I advise all the world to do it. We must *know* before we can *lore*. In order to *know* GOD, we must often *think* of Him; and when we come to *love* Him, we shall then also think of Him often, for our heart will be with our treasure. This is an argument which well deserves your consideration.

I am, Yours, etc.

Tenth Letter

I have had a good deal of difficulty to bring myself to write to Mr. ____, and I do it now purely because you and Madam ____ desire me. Pray write the directions and send it to him. I am very well pleased with the trust which you have in GOD: I wish that He may increase it in you more and more. We cannot have too much in so good and faithful a Friend, who will never fail us in this world nor in the next.

If Mr. ____ makes his advantage of the loss he has had, and puts all his confidence in GOD, He will soon give him another friend, more powerful and more inclined to serve him. He disposes of hearts as He pleases. Perhaps Mr. ____ was too much attached to him he has lost. We ought to love our friends, but without encroaching upon the love due to GOD, which must be the principal.

Pray remember what I have recommended to you, which is, to think often on GOD, by day, by night, in your business, and even in your diversions. He is always near you and with you: leave Him not alone. You would think it rude to leave a friend alone who came to visit you: why then must GOD be neglected? Do not then forget Him, but think on Him often, adore Him continually, live and die with Him; this is the glorious employment of a Christian. In a word, this is our profession; if we do not know it, we must learn it. I will endeavor to help you with my prayers, and am, in our LORD, Yours, etc.

Eleventh Letter

I do not pray that you may be delivered from your pains, but I pray GOD earnestly that He would give you strength and patience to bear them as long as He pleases. Comfort yourself with Him who holds you fastened to the cross. He will loose you when He thinks fit. Happy those who suffer with Him: accustom yourself to suffer in that manner, and seek from Him the strength to endure as much, and as long, as He shall judge to be necessary for you. The men of the world do not comprehend these truths, nor is it to be wondered at, since they suffer like what they are, and not like Christians. They consider sickness as a pain to nature, and not as a favor from GOD; and seeing it only in that light, they find nothing in it but grief and distress. But those who consider sickness as coming from the hand of GOD, as the effect of His mercy, and the means which He employs for their salvation—such, commonly find in it great sweetness and sensible consolation.

I wish you could convince yourself that GOD is often (in some sense) nearer to us, and more effectually present with us, in sickness than in health. Rely upon no other Physician; for, according to my apprehension, He reserves your cure to Himself. Put, then, all your trust in Him, and you will soon find the effects of it in your recovery, which we often retard by putting greater confidence in physic than in GOD.

Whatever remedies you make use of, they will succeed only so far as He permits. When pains come from GOD, He only can cure them. He often sends diseases of the body to cure those of the soul. Comfort yourself with the sovereign Physician both of the soul and body.

Be satisfied with the condition in which GOD places you: however happy you may think me, I envy you. Pains and sufferings would be a paradise to me while I should suffer with my GOD; and the greatest pleasures would be hell to me if I could relish them without Him. All my consolation would be to suffer something for His sake.

I must, in a little time, go to GOD. What comforts me in this life is, that I now see Him *by faith*; and I see Him in such a manner as might make me say sometimes, *I believe no more, but I see.* I feel what faith teaches us, and in that assurance and that practice of faith, I will live and die with Him.

Continue then always with GOD: it is the only support and comfort for your affliction. I shall beseech Him to be with you. I present my service.

Yours, etc.

Twelfth Letter

If we were well accustomed to the exercise of *the presence of* GOD, all bodily diseases would be much alleviated thereby. GOD often permits that we should suffer a little to purify our souls and oblige us to continue *with* Him.

Take courage: offer Him your pains incessantly: pray to Him for strength to endure them. Above all, get a habit of entertaining yourself often with GOD, and forget Him the least you can. Adore Him in your infirmities, offer yourself to Him from time to time, and in the height of your sufferings, beseech Him humbly and affectionately (as a child his father) to make you conformable to His holy-will. I shall endeavor to assist you with my poor prayers.

GOD has many ways of drawing us to Himself. He sometimes hides Himself from us, but *faith* alone, which will not fail us in time of need, ought to be our support, and the foundation of our confidence, which must be all in GOD.

I know not how GOD will dispose of me. I am always happy. All the world suffer; and I, who deserve the severest discipline, feel joys so continual and so great that I can scarce contain them.

I would willingly ask of GOD a part of your sufferings, but that I know my weakness, which is so great, that if He left me one moment to myself I should be the most wretched man alive. And yet I know not how He can leave me alone, because faith gives me as strong a conviction as sense can do, that He never forsakes us until we have first forsaken Him. Let us fear to leave Him. Let us be always with Him. Let us live and die in His presence. Do you pray for me, as I for you.

I am, Yours, etc.

Thirteenth Letter

To the Same .

I am in pain to see you suffer so long. What gives me some
ease and sweetens the feelings I have for your griefs is, that
they are proofs of GOD'S love towards you. See them in that
view and you will bear them more easily. As your case is, it
is my opinion that you should leave off human remedies, and
resign yourself entirely to the providence of GOD: perhaps He
stays only for that resignation and a perfect trust in Him to
cure you. Since, notwithstanding all your cares, physic has
hitherto proved unsuccessful, and your malady still increases,
it will not be tempting GOD to abandon yourself in His
hands, and expect all from Him.

I told you in my last that He sometimes permits bodily
diseases to cure the distempers of the soul. Have courage
then: make a virtue of necessity. Ask of GOD, not deliverance
from your pains, but strength to bear resolutely, for the love
of Him, all that He should please, and as long as He shall
please.

Such prayers, indeed, are a little hard to nature, but most
acceptable to GOD, and sweet to those that love Him. Love
sweetens pains; and when one loves GOD, one suffers for His
sake with joy and courage. Do you so, I beseech you: comfort
yourself with Him, who is the only Physician of all our
maladies. He is the FATHER of the afflicted, always ready to
help us. He loves us infinitely more than we imagine. Love
Him, then, and seek no consolation elsewhere. I hope you will
soon receive it. Adieu. I will help you with my prayers, poor
as they are, and shall always be, in our LORD Yours, etc.

Fourteenth Letter

To the Same

I render thanks to our LORD for having relieved you a little, according to your desire. I have been often near expiring, but I never was so much satisfied as then. Accordingly, I did not pray for any relief, but I prayed for strength to suffer with courage, humility and love. Ah, how sweet it is to suffer with GOD! However great the sufferings may be, receive them with love. It is paradise to suffer and be with Him; so that if in this life we would enjoy the peace of paradise we must accustom ourselves to a familiar, humble, affectionate conversation with Him. We must hinder our spirits wandering from Him upon any occasion. We must make our heart a spiritual temple, wherein to adore Him incessantly. We must watch continually over ourselves, that we may not do, nor say, nor think anything that may displease Him. When our minds are thus employed about GOD, suffering will become full of unction and consolation.

I know that to arrive at this state the beginning is very difficult, for we must act purely in faith. But though it is difficult, we know also that we can do all things with the grace of GOD, which He never refuses to them who ask it earnestly. Knock, persevere in knocking, and I answer for it that He will open to you in His due time, and grant you all at once what He has deferred during many years. Adieu! Pray to Him for me, as I pray to Him for you. I hope to see Him quickly.

I am, Yours, etc.

Fifteenth Letter

To the Same

GOD knoweth best what is needful for us, and all that He does is for our good. If we knew how much He loves us, we should always be ready to receive equally and with indifference from His Hand the sweet and the bitter: all would please that came from Him. The sorest afflictions never appear intolerable, except when we see them in the wrong light. When we see them as dispensed by the hand of GOD, when we know that it is our loving FATHER who abases and distresses us, our sufferings will lose their bitterness, and become even matter of consolation.

Let all our employment be to *know* GOD: the more one *knows* Him, the more one *desires* to know Him. And as *knowledge* is commonly the measure of *love* , the deeper and more extensive our *knowledge* shall be, the greater will be our *love* : and if our love of GOD were great, we should love Him equally in pains and pleasures.

Let us not content ourselves with loving GOD for the mere sensible favors, how elevated soever, which he has done, or may do us. Such favors, though never so great, cannot bring us so near to Him as faith does in one simple act. Let us seek Him often by faith. He is within us: seek Him not elsewhere. If we do love Him alone, are we not rude, and do we not deserve blame, if we busy ourselves about trifles which do not please and perhaps offend Him. It is to be feared these *trifles* will one day cost us dear.

Let us begin to be devoted to Him in good earnest. Let us cast everything besides out of our hearts. He would possess them alone. Beg this favor of Him. If we do what we can on our parts, we shall soon see that change wrought in us which we aspire after. I cannot thank Him sufficiently for the relaxation He has vouchsafed you. I hope from His mercy the favor to see Him within a few days.[4] Let us pray for one another.

I am, in our LORD, Yours, etc.

Notes:

[1]: Gal. i, 10; Eph. vi, 5, 6.

[2]: The particulars which follow are collected from other accounts of Brother Lawrence.

[3]: *I suppose he means* that all distinct notions he could form of GOD, were unsatisfactory, because he perceived them to be unworthy of GOD; and therefore his mind was not to be satisfied but by the views of *faith* , which apprehend GOD as infinite and incomprehensible, as He is in Himself, and not as He can be conceived by human ideas.

[4]: He took to his bed two days after, and died within the week.

Practice and Presence of God
Book II

First Conversation 48
Second Conversation 50
Third Conversation 53
Fourth Conversation 55
First Letter 58
Second Letter 60
Third Letter 62
Fourth Letter 63
Fifth Letter 64
Sixth Letter 67
Seventh Letter 68
Eighth Letter 69
Ninth Letter 70
Tenth Letter 72
Eleventh Letter 73
Twelfth Letter 75
Thirteenth Letter 76

First Conversation

I met Brother Lawrence for the first time today. He told me that God had been especially good to him in his conversion. He was eighteen at the time, and still in the world. He told me that it had all happened one winter day, as he was looking at a barren tree. Although the tree's leaves were indeed gone, he knew that they would soon reappear, followed by blossoms and then fruit. This gave him a profound impression of God's providence and power which never left him. Brother Lawrence still maintains that this impression detached him entirely from the world and gave him such a great love for God that it hasn't changed in all of the forty years he has been walking with Him.

Brother Lawrence had formerly been a servant to the treasurer of the monastery and had been very clumsy. He believed that in order to be saved, he'd have to be punished for this clumsiness. Therefore, he sacrificed all of the pleasures in his life to God. But, rather than punishing him, God gave him nothing but wholehearted satisfaction. Often, he would tell the Lord endearingly that he felt deceived, because his Christian walk had thus far been so pleasant and not filled with suffering as he had anticipated.

Brother Lawrence insisted that it is necessary to always be aware of God's presence by talking with Him throughout each day. To think that you must abandon conversation with Him in order to deal with the world is erroneous. Instead, as we nourish our souls by seeing God in His exaltation, we will derive a great joy at being His.

Another thing he mentioned was that our faith is too weak. Instead of letting faith rule our lives, we are guided by our petty, everyday, mechanical prayers, which are always changing. The Church's only road to the perfection of Christ is faith.

The dear brother remarked that we must give ourselves totally to God, in both temporal and spiritual affairs. Our only happiness should come from doing God's will, whether it brings us some pain or great pleasure. After all, if we're truly devoted to doing God's will, pain and pleasure won't make any difference to us.

We also need to be faithful, even in dry periods. It is during those dry spells that God tests our love for Him. We should take advantage of those times to practice our determination and our surrender to Him. This will often bring us to a maturity further on in our walk with God.

Brother Lawrence wasn't surprised by the amount of sin and unhappiness in the world. Rather, he wondered why there wasn't more, considering the extremes to which the enemy is capable of going. He said he prayed about it, but because he knew God could rectify the situation in a moment if He willed it, he didn't allow himself to become greatly concerned.

To succeed in giving ourselves to God as much as He desires, we must constantly guard our souls. In addition to being involved in spiritual matters, the soul is involved in the things of this world. But when we turn our backs on Him, exposing our souls to the world, He will not so easily answer our call. When we are willing to accept God's help and guard our souls according to His desires, we may commune with Him whenever we like.

Second Conversation

Brother Lawrence said that he was always guided by love. He was never influenced by any other interest, including whether or not he was saved. He was content doing even the smallest chore if he could do it for the love of God. He even found himself quite well off, which he attributed to the fact that he sought only God, and not His gifts. He believed that God is much greater than any of the simple gifts He gives us. Rather than desiring them from Him, he chose to look beyond the gift, hoping to learn more about God Himself. Sometimes he even wished that he could avoid receiving his reward, so that he would have the pleasure of doing something solely for God.

For some years, Brother Lawrence had been quite disturbed because he wasn't certain that he was saved. Even so, he maintained the attitude that he had become a Christian because he loved the Lord, and so he would continueto love Him, whether he was certain of his salvation or not. This way, he would at least have the earthly pleasure of doing everything he could for the love of God. (Later, this uncertainty about his relationship with God left Brother Lawrence.)

After that, he did not dwell on thoughts of heaven or hell. His life was filled with freedom and rejoicing. Lifting all his sins up to God, he tried to show Him how undeserving of His graces he was. But the Lord continued to bless him. Sometimes God even took our brother by the hand and led him before the heavenly court, as if He wished to honor His lowly servant.

In the beginning, Brother Lawrence declared that a little effort was needed to form the habit of continuously conversing with God, telling Him everything that was happening. But after a little careful practice, God's love refreshed him, and it all became quite easy.

Whenever he considered doing some good deed, he always consulted God about it, saying, "Lord, I will never be able to do that if You don't help me." Immediately he would be given more than enough strength.

When he sinned, he confessed it to God with these words: "I can do nothing better without You. Please keep me from falling and correct the mistakes I make." After that he did not feel guilty about the sin.

Brother Lawrence pointed out that he spoke very simply and frankly to God. He asked for help with things as he needed it, and his experience had been that God never failed to respond.

Only recently, Brother Lawrence was asked to go into Burgundy to get supplies for the monastery. This chore was difficult for him, because, first of all, he had no head for business. And, secondly, he was lame in one leg and could not walk on the boat without falling against the cargo of barrels. But neither his awkwardness nor the errand in general caused him any distress. He simply told God that it was His affair, after which he found that everything turned out nicely.

Things went the same way in the kitchen of the monastery, where he worked. Although he once had a great dislike for kitchen work, he developed quite a facility for doing it over the fifteen years he was there. He attributed this to his doing everything for the love of God, asking as often as possible for grace to do his work. He said that he was presently in the shoe repair shop, and that he liked it very much. He would, however, be willing to work anywhere, always rejoicing at being able to do little things for the love of God.

Brother Lawrence was aware of his sins and was not at all surprised by them. "That is my nature," he would say, "the only thing I know how to do." He simply confessed his sins to God, without pleading with Him or making excuses. After this, he was able to peacefully resume his regular activity of love and adoration. If Brother Lawrence didn't sin, he thanked God for it, because only God's grace could keep him from sinning.

When he was troubled by something, he seldom consulted anyone about it. Knowing only that God was present, he walked in the light of faith and was content just to lose himself in God's love no matter what happened. And in God's love, he would find himself again.

He remarked that thinking often spoils everything; that evil usually begins with our thoughts. In Brother Lawrence's opinion, we should reject any thoughts which distract us from serving the Lord or which undermine our salvation. Freeing the mind of such thoughts will permit a comfortable conversation with God. But Brother Lawrence added that this isn't always easy. When he was first saved, he had often spent his entire prayer time rejecting distractions and then falling immediately into them again.

He said that a sharp distinction should be drawn between acts of the intellect and those of the will. The former were of little importance, while the latter meant everything. All we really had to do was to love and rejoice in God. He said that without this love of God good works would not erase a single sin. In fact, God often chose those who had been the greatest sinners to receive His greatest graces, because this would reveal His goodness more dramatically.

Only the blood of Jesus Christ could cleanse us of sin. For this reason, we should strive to love Him with all our hearts. Brother Lawrence said he concentrated on doing little things for Him, since he was unable to do bigger things. After that, anything the Lord willed could happen to him, and he wouldn't be concerned about it. Therefore, he didn't worry about anything, and asked God for nothing except that he might not offend Him.

Third Conversation

Brother Lawrence confided to me that the foundation of his spiritual life was the faith which revealed to him the exalted position of God. Once this became secure in the depths of his heart, he was easily able to do all his actions for the love of God. He truly understood that this solid faith in God was a great honor to Him and gave the Lord an open door to answer his prayers and shower blessings upon him.

He continued that if someone surrenders himself entirely to God, resolving to do anything for Him, the Lord will protect that person from deception. He will also not allow such a person to suffer through trials for very long, but will give him a way of escape that he might endure it (1 Corinthians 10:13).

Brother Lawrence's heartfelt goal was to think of nothing but God. If he did allow some time to pass without thinking of Him, he did not grow upset about it. Once he confessed his weakness to God, he returned to Him with all the more confidence and joy because he had found himself so unhappy apart from God's presence. If he felt any ungracious thought or any temptation generating, he would not panic or feel helpless to resist it. This was because his past experience of God's faithful assistance allowed him to wait until just the right moment to call out. When the time came, he would address himself to God, and the evil thoughts would vanish right away.

Because of this same trust in God's care, when Brother Lawrence had some outside business to attend to, he never worried about it beforehand. Rather, he found God would give him a picture as clear as a mirror image of exactly what to do at precisely the right moment. He had acted in this way for quite some time, without being concerned about something ahead of time. Before he had experienced God's swift help in his affairs, he had attempted to plan every detail, doing the job in his own strength. But now, acting with childlike simplicity in God's sight, he did everything for the love of God, thanking Him for His guidance. And everything he did passed calmly, in a way that held him close to the loving presence of God.

When any outside business unnecessarily diverted him from his communication with God, a little reminder came from the Lord which took possession of his soul, flooding it with the image of God. This sometimes set him on fire to the point that he felt a great impulse to shout praises, to sing, and to dance before the Lord with joy.

Brother Lawrence declared that he felt much closer to God in his day-to-day activities than most people ever believed to be possible.

The worst trial he could imagine was losing his sense of God's presence, which had been with him for so long a time. But his confidence in God's goodness made him certain that He would never leave him entirely. Should he encounter any great difficulty in his life, he knew the Lord would provide the strength he needed to endure it.

With this assurance, Brother Lawrence wasn't afraid of anything. He added that he wasn't afraid of dying to self or losing himself in Christ, because complete surrender to God's will is the only secure road to follow. In it, there is always enough light to assure safe travel.

In the beginning, it is always necessary to be faithful, both in actions and in the renouncing of self. But after that, there is only indescribable joy. If difficulties arise, simply turn to Jesus Christ and pray for His grace, with which everything will become easy.

Our brother remarked that some people go only as far as their regular devotions, stopping there and neglecting love, which is the purpose of those devotions. This could easily be seen in their actions and explained why they possessed so little solid virtue.

Neither skill nor knowledge is needed to go to God, he added. All that is necessary is a heart dedicated entirely and solely to Him out of love for Him above all others.

Fourth Conversation

Today Brother Lawrence spoke to me quite openly and with great enthusiasm about his manner of going to God. He said the most important part lay in renouncing, once and for all, whatever does not lead to God. This would allow us to become involved in a continuous conversation with Him in a simple and unhindered manner.

All we have to do is to recognize God as being intimately present within us. Then we may speak directly to Him every time we need to ask for help, to know His will in moments of uncertainty, and to do whatever He wants us to do in a way that pleases Him. We should offer our work to Him before we begin, and thank Him afterwards for the privilege of having done them for His sake. This continuous conversation would also include praising and loving God incessantly for His infinite goodness and perfection.

Brother Lawrence declared that we ought to ask confidently for God's grace in everything we do, trusting the infinite merits of our Lord rather than our own thoughts. He said that God would never fail to give us His grace, and that he could testify to this personally. This brother in the Lord sinned only when he strayed from God's company, or when he forgot to ask Him for His help.

When we are in doubt, he continued, God never fails to show us the right way to go, as long as our only goal is to please Him and show our love for Him.

He thought it was a shame that some people pursued certain activities (which, he noted, they did rather imperfectly due to human shortcomings), mistaking the means for the end. He said that our sanctification does not depend as much on changing our activities as it does on doing them for God rather than for ourselves.

The most effective way Brother Lawrence had for communicating with God was to simply do his ordinary work. He did this obediently, out of a pure love of God, purifying it as much as was humanly possible. He believed it was a serious mistake to think of our prayer time as being different from any other. Our actions should unite us with God when we are involved in our daily activities, just as our prayer unites us with Him in our quiet time.

He said his prayers consisted totally and simply of God's presence. His soul was resting in God, having lost its awareness of everything but love of Him. When he wasn't in prayer, he felt practically the same way. Remaining near to God, he praised and blessed Him with all his strength. Because of this, his life was full of continual joy.

We must, Brother Lawrence remarked, trust in God and surrender completely to Him. He will not deceive us. Never tire of doing even the smallest things for Him, because He isn't impressed so much with the dimensions of our work as with the love in which it is done. And we should not be discouraged if we fail in the beginning. The practice would eventually cause our efforts to become a pleasurable habit that we would do without thinking.

He said that in order to be sure we were doing God's will, we should simply develop an attitude of faith, hope, and love. We need not be concerned about anything else. It simply is not important, and should only be regarded as the means of getting to the final goal of being entirely lost in the love of God. We should desire to love Him as perfectly as we can, in this life as well as in Eternity. Many things are possible for the person who has hope. Even more is possible for the person who has faith. And still more is possible for the person who knows how to love. But everything is possible for the person who practices all three virtues.

Brother Lawrence added that when we begin our Christian walk, we must remember that we have been living in the world, subject to all sorts of miseries, accidents and poor dispositions from within. The Lord will cleanse and humble us in order to make us more like Christ. As we go through this cleansing process, we will grow closer to God.

Therefore, we should rejoice in our difficulties, bearing them as long as the Lord wills, because only through such trials will our faith become purified, more precious than gold (1 Peter 1:7; 4:19).

First Letter

Dear friend,

I'd like to use this occasion to inform you of the thoughts of one of our brothers concerning the wonderful results and the continual help he receives from the presence of God. We could both profit from them. [It is believed that Brother Lawrence was referring to himself in the following. His humility restrained him from saying so.]

For more than forty years, this brother's principal endeavor has been to stay as close as possible to God, doing, saying, and thinking nothing that might displease Him. He has no reason for doing this, except to show his gratitude for God's pure love, and because God deserves infinitely more than that anyway.

This brother has become so accustomed to God's Divine presence that he relies on it for help on all sorts of occasions. His soul has been filled with a constant inner joy that is sometimes so overwhelming, he feels compelled to do what may seem to some as childish things, in order to prevent the feeling from becoming too intense.

If he sometimes strays from this Divine presence, God immediately recalls him by communicating with him through the Holy Spirit. This often happens to him when he is busiest with his work. He responds faithfully to God's calling, either by offering his heart to God, by a tender, loving look, or by some affectionate words, such as, "My God, I am all Yours; do what You will with me." Then, it is almost as if this God of love returns to his soul to rest again, satisfied with these few words. Experiencing these things makes this brother certain beyond all doubt that God is always in the depth of his soul, no matter what he does or what happens to him.

Imagine what contentment and satisfaction he enjoys, possessing such an ever-present treasure! He isn't anxious to find it and doesn't worry about where to look for it, because he has already found it and may take whatever he wants from it.

He often calls men blind, complaining that we are content with too little. God has infinite treasures to give us, he says. Why should we be satisfied with a brief moment of worship? With such meager devotion, we restrain the flow of God's abundant grace. If God can find a soul filled with a lively faith, He pours His grace into it in a torrent which, having found an open channel, gushes out exuberantly.

We often stop this torrent by our lack of respect for it. But we mustn't restrain it any longer. Let us go into our hearts, dear friend, breaking down the dike, making way for grace, and making up for lost time! You and I are getting along in years. We may have little time left to live. Death is always near, so be prepared, for we only die once.

Once again, let us examine our inner selves. Time is pressing down on us, and each of us must be responsible for himself. I believe you have prepared yourself properly, so you won't be taken by surprise. I respect you for this; it is, after all, our business to be as open as possible to God's grace. However, we must continuously walk in God's Spirit, since in the spirit-life not to advance is to fall back. But those who have the wind of the Holy Spirit in their souls glide ahead even while they sleep. If the vessel of our soul is still being tossed by winds or storms, we should wake the Lord Who has been resting with us all along, and He will swiftly calm the sea.

I have taken the liberty, my dear friend, of telling you all this so you might reexamine your own relationship with God. If by some means (I pray it is not so), it has cooled even slightly, perhaps our bother's attitude will rekindle and inflame it. Do you remember our first enthusiasm and love for God? We could both recall it by way of this bother's example. He isn't well-known, in worldly terms, but with God he is tenderly loved and caressed. Let us pray earnestly for one another to receive this grace for ourselves.

Second Letter

My dear friend,

Today I received two books and a letter from a mutual friend who is preparing to commit her whole life in service to the Lord. She has asked for both of our prayers as she makes her firm resolution to live her life for Him.

I am sending you one of the books which discusses the importance of God's presence, so you know that it is close to my heart.

I still believe that all spiritual life consists of practicing God's presence, and that anyone who practices it correctly will soon attain spiritual fulfillment.

To accomplish this, it is necessary for the heart to be emptied of everything that would offend God. He wants to possess your heart completely. Before any work can be done in your soul, God must be totally in control.

There is no sweeter manner of living in the world than continuous communion with God. Only those who have experienced it can understand. However, I don't advise you to practice it for the sole purpose of gaining consolation for your problems. Seek it, rather, because God wills it and out of love for Him.

If I were a preacher, I would preach nothing but practicing the presence of God. If I were to be responsible for guiding souls in the right direction, I would urge everyone to be aware of God's constant presence, if for no other reason than because His presence is a delight to our souls and spirits.

It is, however, also necessary. If we only knew how much we need God's grace, we would never lose touch with Him. Believe me. Make a commitment never to deliberately stray from Him, to live the rest of your life in His holy presence. Don't do this in expectation of receiving heavenly comforts; simply do it out of love for Him.

Put your hand to the task! If you do it right, you will soon see the results. I will support you with my prayers. Please keep me in your prayers, also, and in the prayers of your church.

Third Letter

Dear friend,

I'm amazed that you haven't let me know your opinion of the book I sent you. You must have received it by now. Practice it energetically, even in your old age. It truly is better late than never.

I honestly cannot understand how people who claim to love the Lord can be content without practicing His presence. My preference is to retire with Him to the deepest part of my soul as often as possible. When I am with Him there, nothing frightens me. But the slightest diversion away from Him is painful to me.

Spending time in God's presence doesn't weaken the body. Leaving the seemingly innocent and permissible pleasures of the world for a time will, on the contrary, give us comfort. In fact, God won't allow a soul that is searching for Him to be comforted anywhereother than with Him. So it makes sense to sacrifice ourselves for some time in His presence.

This does not mean that you have to suffer in this endeavor. No, God must be served with holy freedom. He should labor faithfully, without distress or anxiety, calmly recalling our spirit to God whenever it is distracted.

The only requirement is that we place our confidence entirely in God. Abandon any other concerns, including any special devotions you've undertaken simply as a means to an end. God is our "end." If we are diligently practicing His presence, we shouldn't need our former "means." We can continue our exchange of love with Him by just remaining in His holy presence. Adore Him and praise Him! There are so many ways we can thank Him. The Holy Spirit dwelling in us leads us to love God in a diversity of ways.

God be with all of you.

Fourth Letter

My dear sister in the Lord,

I sympathize with your difficult situation. I think that freeing yourself of your present responsibilities for a while and devoting yourself entirely to prayer would be the best thing you could do for yourself. God does not ask much of us. But remembering Him, praising Him, asking for His grace, offering Him your troubles, or thanking Him for what He has given you will console you all the time. During your meals or during any daily duty, lift your heart up to Him, because even the least little remembrance will please Him. You don't have to pray out loud; He's nearer than you can imagine.

It isn't necessary that we stay in church in order to remain in God's presence. We can make our heart a chapel where we can go anytime to talk to God privately. These conversations can be so loving and gentle, and anyone can have them.

So why not begin? He may be waiting for us to take the first step. Because we have such a short time to live, we should spend our remaining time with God. Even suffering will be easier when we are with Him, but without Him, even the greatest pleasures will be joyless. May He be blessed in everything! Gradually train yourself to show your love for Him by asking for His grace. Offer your heart to Him at every moment. Don't restrict your love of Him with rules or special devotions. Go out in faith, with love and humility.

I remain your servant in the Lord.

Fifth Letter

Dear Reverend,

I would like very much to know your opinion of my current situation. A few days ago, I was talking to a friend of mine about spiritual life. This friend described it as a life of grace, which begins with the fear and respect of a servant, growing through the hope of eternal life, finally to find fullness in pure love. She also said that different people experience this consummate love to greater and lesser degrees.

I haven't followed any particular steps in my own spiritual growth. On the contrary, I found methods to be discouraging. My intent, at the beginning of my Christian walk, was to give myself to God all at once. I did this out of love for Him, because I wanted to pay for my sins and renounce everything that offended Him.

My first prayers were about death, judgment, hell, heaven, and my sins. This went on for several years. When I wasn't praying, I
kept myself carefully in God's presence, even while I was working. I knew He was always near me, in the deepest part of my heart. This gave me such great respect for God that I was content with faith alone. And so I continued to pray this way, which gave me enormous peace and joy.

During the first ten years, however, I worried that my walk with the Lord wasn't good enough. Because I couldn't forget my past sins, I felt very guilty when I thought of all the grace He had shown me. During this time, I used to fall often and then get up again. It seemed that everything even God was against me, and that only faith was on my side. Sometimes I believed I felt this way because I was trying to show, at the beginning of my walk, the same maturity it had taken other Christians years to achieve. Soetimes it got so bad that I thought I was on my way to hell— willfully offending God — and that there wee no salvation for me.

Thankfully, these worries did not weaken my faith in God, but actually made it stronger. When I finally reached the point where I expected the rest of my life to be very difficult; I suddenly found myself wholly changed. My soul, which had always been troubled, finally came to rest in a profound inner peace.

Since that time, I have been serving God simply, in humility and faith. Out of love, I try not to say do, or think anything that might offend Him. My only request is that He do whatever He pleases with me.

I feel unable to express what is going on inside me right now. I'm not anxious about my purpose in life, because I only want to do God's will. I wouldn't even lift a straw from the ground against His order or for any other motive than love for Him. Pure love of Him is all that keeps me going.

I have given up all but my intercessory prayers to focus my attention on remaining in His holy presence. I keep my attention on God in a simple, loving way. This is my soul's secret experience of the actual, unceasing presence of God. It gives me such contentment and joy, that I sometimes feel compelled to do rather childish things to control it.

To sum up, kind sir, I am sure that my soul has been with God for more than thirty years. I consider God my King, against Whom I've committed all sorts of crimes. Confessing my sins to Him and asking Him to forgive me, I place myself in His hands to do whatever He pleases with me.

This King, Who is full of goodness and mercy, doesn't punish me. Rather, He embraces me lovingly and invites me to eat at His table. He serves me Himself and gives me the keys to His treasury, treating me as His favorite. He converses with me without mentioning my sins or my forgiveness. My former habits are seemingly forgotten. Although I beg Him to do whatever He wishes with me, He does nothing but caress me. This is what being in His holy presence is like.

My day-to-day life consists of giving God my simple, loving attention. If I'm distracted, He calls me back in tones that are supernaturally beautiful. If you think of me, remember the grace with which God has blessed me, rather than my typically human ineptitude.

My prayers consist of a simple continuation of this same exercise. Sometimes I imagine that I'm a piece of stone, waiting for the sculptor. When I give myself to God this way, He begins sculpting my soul into the perfect image of His beloved Son. At other times, I feel my whole mind and heart being raised up into God's presence, as if, without effort, they had always belonged there.

Some people may consider this attitude selfdeceptive. But I cannot permit it to be called deception, since in this state of enjoying God I desire nothing but His presence. If I am deceiving myself, the Lord will have to remedy it. I want Him to do whatever He pleases with me; all I want is to be completely His.

Your suggestions as to how I should handle all of this will help me, because I respect your opinion very much.

I remain yours in Christ.

Sixth Letter

Dear sister,

As I promised, I am praying for you, even though my prayers are meager. Wouldn't we be happy if we could find the full treasure described in the Gospel? Nothing else would matter. It is infinite; the more we explore it, the more riches we will find. May we never stop searching until we have found all of it!

I don't know what's to become of me. It seems that a tranquil soul and a quiet spirit come to me even while I sleep. Because I am at rest, the trials of life bring me no suffering. I don't know what God has in store for me, but I feel so serene that it doesn't matter. What do I have to be afraid of when I'm with Him? I stay with Him as much as I can. May He be blessed for everything! Amen.

Seventh Letter

Dear friend,

We have a God Who is infinitely good and Who knows what He is doing. He will come and deliver you from your present trouble in His perfect time and when you may least expect it. Hope in Him more than ever. Thank Him for the strength and patience He is giving you, even in the midst of this trial, for it is an evident mark of His concern for you. Encourage yourself with His love and thank Him for everything.

I admire the strength and courage of your friend, the soldier. God has given him a fine character, even though he is still a little worldly and immature. I hope that the problems God has allowed him to have will cause him to become more concerned about his spiritual life. Encourage him to put all his confidence in God, Who is always with him. He should communicate with God at all times, especially in the greatest dangers.

Lifting our hearts up to God is sufficient. Remembering Him briefly or praising Him even in the midst of battle is very pleasing to God. And, far from destroying a soldier's courage, this should strengthen him.

Tell him to dwell in God as much as possible, gradually getting used to this simple, but holy, exercise. No one will be able to see it. And besides, nothing is easier than praising the Lord.

Tell him to do this as often as he can. It is quite acceptable behavior for a soldier; in fact, it is necessary for someone whose life (and salvation) are constantly in danger.

I pray that God will help him, and all of his family, whom I salute.

Eighth Letter

Dear friend,

You aren't the only one to be distracted from the presence of God; I understand completely. Our minds are so flighty. But remember that our God-given will governs all of our strength. It must recall the mind to God. Otherwise, our spirit may wander, dragging us down to the things of this earth.

I think the remedy for the problem is to confess our faults to God and humble ourselves before Him. It isn't necessary to be too verbose in prayer, because lengthy prayers encourage wandering thoughts. Simply present yourself to God as if you were a poor man knocking on the door of a rich man, and fix your attention on His presence. If your mind wanders at times, don't be upset, because being upset will only distract you more. Allow your will to recall your attention gently to God. Such perseverance will please Him.

Another way to prevent the mind from wandering away from God during prayer is to train yourself to dwell in His presence all day long. This will provide a sort of "practice" for you, as you remind yourself to concentrate on Him. Remaining in His presence during prayer time will thus become easier.

You know from my other letters how advantageous I think it is to practice the presence of God. Let us take this act of loving God seriously, and pray for one another.

I remain your brother in Christ.

Ninth Letter

Dear friend,

Here is the answer to the letter I received from our dear sister in the Lord; please give it to her. She seems so full of good will, but she wants to go faster than grace allows. It is not possible to become spiritually mature all at once. I recommend that you work with her, because we should help each other with our advice and, even more, with our good example. I'd appreciate your sending me news of her from time to time, so that I may know how she is coming along.

Let us often remember, my dear friend, that our sole occupation in life is to please God. What meaning can anything else have? You and I have walked with the Lord for more than forty years. Have we really used those years to love and serve God, Who, by His mercy, called us for that purpose? When I consider the blessings God has given, and still continues to give I feel ashamed. I feel I have abused those blessings, barely using them profitably to become more like Christ.

But God in His mercy gives us a little more time. We can begin all over again and repair the lost opportunity, returning with complete confidence to this kind Father, Who is always ready to receive us lovingly. Abandon everything that isn't of God. Doesn't He deserve this and much more? Think of Him continually, and put all your confidence in Him. Soon His abundant grace will engulf us. With it, we can do anything, but without it, we can commit only sin.

We cannot avoid the dangers of life without God's continual help, so we should ask Him for it ceaselessly. But how can we ask for help unless we are with Him? To be with Him, we must cultivate the holy habit of thinking of Him often.

You will tell me that I always say the same thing. What can I say? It is true. I don't know an easier method, nor do I practice any other, so I advise this one to everybody. We have to know someone before we can truly love them. In order to know God, we must think about Him often. And once we get to know Him, we will think about Him even more often, because where our treasure is, there also is our heart!

Tenth Letter

Dear Madame,

It was difficult for me to decide whether or not to write to our brother in the Lord. I do so only because you wish it. Would you mind addressing and sending the letter yourself?

Your confidence in God is beautiful; may He bless you for it. We can never trust this Friend of ours too much. He is so good and so faithful not to fail us, neither in this world nor in the next.

I pray that our brother is wise enough to profit from his loss and to trust God completely. Perhaps our Lord will give him another friend who is more powerful and better disposed. After all, God deals with our hearts according to His will.

There may have been too much of the world in his love. He may have been too attached to the one he lost. Even though we should love our friends, that love shouldn't hinder our love of God, Who must be first.

Remember what I advised you to do: Think about God as often as you can, day and night, in everything you do. He is always with you. Just as you would be rude if you left a friend who was visiting you alone, why abandon God and leave Him alone?

Do not forget Him! Think of Him often; adore Him ceaselessly; live and die with Him. That is the real business of a Christian; in a word, it is our profession. If we do not know it, we must learn it. I will pray for you.

Eleventh Letter

Dear friend,

Since you are so seriously interested in knowing how I attained the ability God granted me to dwell in His presence, I will try to explain it. But I must ask you not to show my letter to anyone. If I thought you were going to let someone else read it, I would not discuss the matter, despite all of my desire for your spiritual growth.

Although I found several books describing how to know God and mature spiritually, I believed they would only serve to confuse my soul. What I wanted was simply to belong totally to God. So I decided to give everything I could give in order to attain the greatest blessing in return, knowing Him. I gave myself completely to God, accepting His forgiveness of my sins, after which I renounced everything that would offend Him. I began to live as if there were no one but God and myself in the world.

Sometimes I thought of myself as a criminal standing before Him, my Judge; at other times I regarded Him as my Father. I tried to keep my heart in this father/child relationship as much as I could, adoring Him there. I held my spirit in His holy presence, recalling it whenever it went astray. This exercise was rather difficult. Yet, I was able to continue it without being disturbed when I was involuntarily distracted. It occupied as much time during my regular working day as it did my prayer time. At all times — every hour and every minute — I drove everything out of my spirit that might take me from the thought of God.

This has been my everyday routine since I began my walk with the Lord. Although sometimes I practice it timidly and with a great many mistakes, I am still quite blessed by it. This has to be due to the great goodness and mercy of God. We can indeed do nothing without Him (which is truer for me than for others). But when we faithfully keep ourselves in His holy presence and always remember that He is before us, we avoid offending Him (at least voluntarily). Then, we may take the holy liberty of asking Him for the grace we need. By continuing this practice of His presence, He becomes more familiar to us, and His presence becomes a natural thing.

Thank God for His goodness to us!

Twelfth Letter

Hello friend!

Take courage! God often allows us to go through difficulties to purify our souls and to teach us to rely on Him more (1 Peter 1:6-7). So offer Him your problems unceasingly, and ask Him for the strength to overcome them. Talk to Him often; forget Him as seldom as possible. Praise Him. When the difficulties are at their worst, go to Him humbly and lovingly as a child goes to a loving father and ask for the help you need from His grace. I will support you with my humble prayers.

God has various ways of drawing us to Him. But sometimes He hides from us. In those times, the sole support of our confidence must be our faith, which must be totally in God. Such faith will not fail.

Remember that God never leaves us unless we go away first. We should be careful never to separate ourselves from His presence. We must dwell with Him always; so let us live with Him now and die with Him when our time is at hand. Pray to Him for me, and I will for you. I remain yours in our Lord.

Thirteenth Letter

Dear friend,

I cannot thank God enough for the way He has begun to deliver you from your trial.

God knows very well what we need and that all He does is for our good. If we knew how much He loves us, we would always be ready to face life — both its pleasures and its troubles.

You know, the difficulties of life do not have to be unbearable. It is the way that we look at them through faith or unbelief. We must be convinced that our Father is full of love for us and that He only permits trials to come our way for our own good.

Let us occupy ourselves entirely in knowing God. The more we know Him, the more we will desire to know Him. As love increases with knowledge, the more we know God, the more we will truly love Him. And we will learn to love Him equally in times of distress or in times of great joy.

Although we seek and love God because of the blessings He has given us, or for those He may give us in the future, let us not stop there. These blessings, as great es they are, will never carry us as near to Him as a simple act of faith does in a time of need or trouble.

Let us look to God with these eyes of faith. He is within us; we don't need to seek Him elsewhere. We have only ourselves to blame if we turn from God, occupying ourselves instead with the trifles of life. In the Lord's patience, He endures our weaknesses. But just think of the price we pay by being separated from His presence!

Once and for all, let us begin to be His entirely. Let us banish from our heart and soul all that does not reflect Jesus. Let us ask Him for the grace to do this, so that He alone might rule in our hearts.

I must confide in you, my dear friend, that I hope, in His grace, that I will see Him in a few days.

Let us pray to Him for one another.

[Brother Lawrence passed from this life into the next just a few days later, on February 12, 1691, to dwell fully, in the presence of his God.

Spiritual Maxims

Spiritual Maxims 81
Practice Necessary to Acquire the Spiritual Life 82
How to Adore God in Spirit and in Truth 84
The Union of the Soul with God 85
The Presence of God 86
The Means of Acquiring the Presence of God 87
The Blessings of the Presence of God 88

Spiritual Maxims

All things are possible to him who believes; still more to him who hopes; still more to him who loves; and most of all to him who practices all three. All of those who are baptized and believe as they should have taken the first step toward perfection. They will attain perfection if they practice the following maxims.

1. We should be considerate of God in everything we do and say. Our goal should be to become perfect in our adoration of Him throughout this earthly life in preparation for all eternity. We must make a firm resolution to overcome, with God's grace, all the difficulties encountered in a spiritual life.

2. From the very beginning of our Christian walk, we should remember who we are and that we are unworthy of the name of Christian, except for what Christ has done for us. In cleansing us from all our impurities, God desires to humble us and allow us to go through a number of trials or difficulties.

3. We must believe with certainty that it is both pleasing to God and good for us to sacrifice ourselves for Him. Without this complete submission of our hearts and minds to His will, He cannot work in us to make us perfect.

4. The more we aspire to be perfect, the more dependent we are on the grace of God. We begin to need His help with every little thing and at every moment, because without it we can do nothing. The world, the flesh, and the devil wage a fierce and continuous war on our souls. If we weren't capable of humbly depending on God for assistance, our souls would be dragged down. Although this total dependence may sometimes go against our human nature, God takes great pleasure in it. That should bring us rest

Practice Necessary to Acquire the Spiritual Life

1. The most holy and necessary practice in our spiritual life is the presence of God. That means finding constant pleasure in His divine company, speaking humbly and lovingly with Him in all seasons, at every moment, without limiting the conversation in any way. This is especially important in times of temptation, sorrow, separation from God, and even in times of unfaithfulness and sin.

2. We must try to converse with God in little ways while we do our work; not in memorized prayer, not trying to recite previously formed thoughts. Rather, we should purely and simply reveal our hearts as the words come to us.

3. We must do everything with great care, avoiding impetuous actions, which are evidence of a disordered spirit. God wishes us to work gently, calmly, and lovingly with Him, asking Him to accept our work. By this continual attention to God, we will "resist the devil and cause him to flee" (James 4:7).

4. Whatever we do, even if we are reading the Word or praying, we should stop for a few minutes — as often as possible — to praise God from the depths of our hearts, to enjoy Him there in secret. Since you believe that God is always with you, no matter what you may be doing, why shouldn't you stop for awhile to adore Him, to praise Him, to petition Him, to offer Him your heart, and to thank Him? What could please God more than for us to leave the cares of the world temporarily in order to worship Him in our spirits? These momentary retreats serve to free us from our selfishness, which can only exist in the world. In short, we cannot show God our loyalty to Him more than by renouncing our worldly selves as much as a thousand times a day to enjoy even a single moment with Him.

This doesn't mean you must leave the duties of the world forever; that would be impossible. Let prudence be your guide. But I do believe that it is a common mistake of spirit-filled persons not to leave the cares of the world from time to time to praise God in their spirits and to rest in the peace of His divine presence for a few moments.

5. Our adoration of God should be done in faith, believing that He really lives in our hearts, and that He must be loved and served in spirit and in truth. Believe that He is the most independent One, upon Whom all of us depend, and that He is aware of everything that happens to us.

The Lord's perfections are truly beyond measure. By His infinite excellence and His sovereign place as both Creator and Savior, He has the right to possess us and all that exists in both heaven and earth. It should be His good pleasure to do with each of us whatever He chooses through all time and eternity. Because of all He is to us, we owe Him our thoughts, words and actions. Let us earnestly endeavor to do this.

6. We must carefully examine ourselves to see which virtues we are in most need of, and which we find the hardest to acquire. We should also take note of the sins that we most frequently fall into and what occasions often contribute to that fall. It is in our times of struggle with these areas that we can go before God with entire confidence and remain firm in the presence of His divine Majesty. In humble adoration, we must confess to Him our sins and weaknesses, lovingly asking for the help of His grace in our time of need. In this way, we will find that we can partake of all the virtues found in Him, even though we do not possess one of our own.

How to Adore God in Spirit and in Truth

There are three points to consider here:

First, to adore God in Spirit and in truth means to adore Him as we should. Because God is a Spirit, He must be adored in spirit. That is to say, we must worship Him with a humble, sincere love that comes from the depth and center of our soul. Only God can see this adoration, which we must repeat until it becomes part of our nature, as if God were one with our soul and our soul were one with God. Practice will demonstrate this.

Secondly, to adore God in truth is to recognize Him for what He is, and ourselves for what we are. Adoring God in truth means that our heart actually sees God as infinitely perfect and worthy of our praise. What man, regardless of how little sense he may have, would not exert all his strength to show his respect and love of this great God?

Thirdly, to adore God in truth is to admit that our nature is just the opposite of His. Yet, He is willing to make us like Him, if we desire it. Who would be so rash as to neglect, even for a moment, the respect, the love, the service, and the continual adoration that we owe Him?

The Union of the Soul with God

The first way in which the soul is united with God is through salvation, solely by His grace.

This is followed by a period in which a saved soul comes to know God through a series of experiences, some of which bring it into closer union with Him and some take it further away. The soul learns which activities bring God's presence nearer. It remains in His presence by practicing those activities.

The most perfect union with God is the actual presence of God. Although this relationship with God is totally spiritual, it is quite dynamic, because the soul is not asleep, but powerfully excited. It is livelier than fire and brighter than the unclouded sun. Yet, it is at the same time tender and devout. It is not a simple expression of the heart, like saying, "Lord, I love You with all my heart," or other similar words. Rather, it is an inexpressible state of the soul — gentle, peaceful, respectful, humble, loving, and very simple — that urges it to love God, to adore Him, and to embrace Him with both tenderness and joy.

Everyone who is striving for divine union must realize that just because something is agreeable and delightful to the will does not mean that it will bring one closer to God. Sometimes it is helpful to disengage the sentiments of the will from the world, in order that it can focus entirely on God. For if the will is able in some manner to comprehend Him, it can be only by love. And that love, which has its end in God, will be hindered by the things of this world.

The Presence of God

The presence of God is the concentration of the soul's attention on God, remembering that He is always present.

I know a person who for forty years has practiced the presence of God, to which he gives several other names. Sometimes he calls it a simple act — a clear and distinct knowledge of God, and sometimes he calls it a vague view or a general and loving look at God — a remembrance of Him. He also refers to it as attention to God, silent communion with God, confidence in God, or the life and the peace of the soul. To sum it up, this person has told me that all these manners of the presence of God are synonyms which signify the same thing, which have all become natural to him.

My friend says that by dwelling in the presence of God he has established such a sweet communion with the Lord that his spirit abides, without much effort, in the restful peace of God. In this rest, he is filled with a faith that equips him to handle anything that comes to him.

This is what he calls the "actual presence" of God, which includes any and all kinds of communion a person who still dwells on the earth can possibly have with God in heaven. At times, he can live as if no one else existed on earth but himself and God. He lovingly speaks with God wherever he goes, asking Him for all he needs and rejoicing with Him in a thousand ways.

Nevertheless, one should realize that this conversation with God occurs in the depth and center of the soul. It is there that the soul speaks to God heart to heart and always dwells in a great and profound peace that the soul enjoys in God. The trouble that happens in the world can become like a blaze of straw that goes out even as it is catching fire. The soul can retain its interior peace in God.

The presence of God is, then, the life and nourishment of the soul, which can be acquired with the grace of God. Here are the means to do so.

The Means of Acquiring the Presence of God

1. The first means is a new life, received by salvation through the blood of Christ.

2. The second is faithfully practicing God's presence. This must always be done gently, humbly, and lovingly, without giving way to anxiety or problems.

3. The soul's eyes must be kept on God, particularly when something is being done in the outside world. Since much time and effort are needed to perfect this practice, one should not be discouraged by failure. Although the habit is difficult to form, it is a source of divine pleasure once it is learned. It is proper that the heart — which is the first to live and which dominates all the other parts of the body — should be the first and the last to love God. The heart is the beginning and the end of all our spiritual and bodily actions and, generally speaking, of everything we do in our lives. It is, therefore, the heart whose attention we must carefully focus on God.

4. In the beginning of this practice, it would not be wrong to offer short phrases that are inspired by love, such as "Lord, I am all Yours," "God of love, I love You with all my heart," or "Lord, use me according to Your will." But remember to keep the mind from wandering or returning to the world. Hold your attention on God alone by exercising your will to remain in God's presence.

5. Although this exercise may be difficult at first to maintain, it has marvelous effects on the soul when it is faithfully practiced. It draws the graces of the Lord down in abundance and shows the soul how to see God's presence everywhere with a pure and loving vision, which is the holiest, firmest, easiest, and the most effective attitude for prayer.

The Blessings of the Presence of God

1. The first blessing that the soul receives from the practice of the presence of God is that its faith is livelier and more active everywhere in our lives. This is particularly true in difficult times, since it obtains the grace we need to deal with temptation and to conduct ourselves in the world. The soul accustomed by this exercise to the practice of faith can actually see and feel God by simply entering His presence. It envokes Him easily and obtains what it needs. In so doing, the soul could be said to approach the Blessed, in that it can almost say, "I no longer believe, but I see and experience." Its faith becomes more and more penetrating as it advances through practice.

2. The practice of the presence of God strengthens us in hope. Our hope increases as our faith penetrates God's secrets through practice of our holy exercise. The soul discovers in God a beauty infinitely surpassing not only that of bodies that we see on earth, but even that of the angels. Our hope increases and grows stronger, and the amount of good that it expects to enjoy, and that in some degree it tastes, reassures and sustains it.

3. This practice causes the will to rejoice at being set apart from the world, setting it aglow with the fire of holy love. This is because the soul is always with God, Who is a consuming fire, Who reduces into powder whatever is opposed to Him. The soul thus inflamed can no longer live except in the presence of its God. This presence produces a holy ardor, a sacred urgency, and a violent desire in the heart to see this God, Who is loved.

4. By practicing God's presence and continuously looking at Him, the soul familiarizes itself with Him to the extent that it passes almost its whole life in continual acts of love, praise, confidence, thanksgiving, offering, and petition. Sometimes all this may merge into one single act that does not end, because thesoul is always in the ceaseless exercise of God's Divine presence.

The Life of Brother Lawrence
By Joseph de Beaufort

A truth which constantly recurs in Holy Scripture is that the arm of God is not shortened, since His mercy cannot be exhausted by our miseries. The power of His grace is no less great today than it was in the first days of the Church. God wished to keep saints for Himself until the end of the world. These saints would pay Him a respect worthy of His grandeur and majesty and would be models of virtue because of the holy example they set.

God was not content to have these extraordinary men born in the early centuries only. He still raises up men who perfectly fulfill these two duties of a saint, and who guard the fruits of the Spirit in themselves, transmit them, and make them live again in others.

Such a man was Brother Lawrence of the Resurrection, a Carmelite lay-brother. God caused him to be born in these latter days to reverence Him and to provide an example of the faithful practice of all the virtues.

His worldly name was Nicholas Herman. His father and his mother, upright people who led an exemplary life, taught him in his childhood to love the Lord. They were particularly careful about his education, giving him only those lessons which were consistent with the Gospel.

When he was a young man, he joined the armed services. Conducting himself with simplicity and honesty, he began to receive evidence from God of His goodness and His mercy.

To begin with, he was taken prisoner by a small body of German troops and treated as a spy. Who can imagine how far his patience and calmness went during this disagreeable event? They even threatened to hang him. But he simply answered that he was not what they supposed, adding that, since he had never done anything to give him a bad conscience, death didn't frighten him anyway. When the officers in charge heard this, they released him.

Later, our young soldier was wounded, and his injury forced him to retire to the home of his parents, who were not far away. This gave him the opportunity to undertake a more holy profession — fighting under the banner of Jesus Christ.

He resolved to give himself wholly to God and to repair his past conduct, not because of vanity, but through sentiments of true devotion. God then allowed him to perceive the nothingness of the pleasures of the world and touched him with a love of heavenly things.

Not realizing the fullness of God's grace, Brother Lawrence did not allow that grace to immediately alleviate his problems. He struggled with serious concerns about his profession, the corruption of the world, man's instability and infidelity, and the treason of enemies. The eternal truth of the Lord, however, finally allowed him to conquer those fears. He made a firm resolution to accept the teachings of the Gospel and walk in the footprints of Jesus Christ.

This brought a new light to his countenance. It freed him from the difficulties that the devil and the world normally put in the path of those who wish to give their lives to the Lord. Our brother acquired a prudent firmness that gave him such a strong determination to follow God that all his former difficulties were washed away in a moment, as if by a miracle. Meditating on the promises of the Lord and his love for Jesus Christ changed him into another man. The humility of the cross became more desirable to him than all the glory the world had to offer.

Filled with a divine zeal, Brother Lawrence sought God in the simplicity and the sincerity of his heart. Because his soul was weary of the painful life it had been leading up to that time in the world, he decided to retire to the desert. There, through his new Christian strength, he was able to get closer to God than he had ever been.

But such a solitary life is not good for young Christians, which our brother soon discovered. Seeing how joy, then sadness; peace, then anxiety; confidence, then heaviness took turns ruling his soul, Brother Lawrence began to doubt the wisdom of his decision to live in the desert, wishing instead to live within a Christian brotherhood. Life within such a group would be based on the firm rock of Jesus Christ, rather than on the shifting sands of temporary, individual devotion. And the members of the group could edify and exhort one another, protecting themselves against the changeableness of their individual whims. Although the first step was difficult, he was lovingly persuaded by God to go to Paris, where he became a lay-brother of the Carmelite Order and took the name of Brother Lawrence. From the very beginning, prayer was of particular importance to him. No matter how much work he had to do, he never cut his prayer time short. Recalling God's presence and the love which resulted from it soon made him the model of his fellow-classmates in the monastery. Although he was assigned the humblest duties there, he never complained. The grace of Jesus Christ sustained him in everything that was unpleasant or tiresome.

His faithfulness to God was exemplary. Even when mistakenly told by one of his superiors that there was talk of dismissing him from the monastery, he replied: "I am in the hands of God; He will do with me as He pleases. If I do not serve Him here, I will serve Him elsewhere."

However, as Brother Lawrence attempted to move into a more spiritual life, memories of the sins of his past life engulfed him, and he judged himself a great sinner, unworthy of any of God's attentions. This led to ten years of intense fear and anxiety in which he often doubted his salvation. With an afflicted heart, he would pour out his troubles to God. But his own fears of what it would cost to serve God completely caused him to resist God's total salvation.

In this bitter, dark time, Brother Lawrence found little comfort in prayer, but he continued to pray, nevertheless. Placing his trust in God, his uppermost desire was still to please Him. Even when he felt he should give it up completely, he found the inner strength and courage to endure. Finally, he cried out to God, "It no longer matters to me what I do or what I suffer, provided that I remain lovingly united to Your will."

This is precisely the disposition God wanted him to acquire before pouring out the blessings of His presence. What our humble brother had not known was just how merciful God is toward sinners such as himself. He didn't realize he had already been forgiven. But from that moment on, the firmness of his soul grew greater than ever. God, Who can accomplish wondrous things in a moment, suddenly opened Brother Lawrence's eyes. He received a divine revelation of

God's majesty that illuminated his spirit, dissipated all his fears, and ended his inner struggles and pain. From that moment, meditating on the character and lovingkindness of God molded Brother Lawrence's character. It became so natural to him that he passed the last forty years of his life in continuous practice of the presence of God, which he described as a quiet, familiar conversation with Him.

Brother Lawrence began this practice by cultivating a deep presence of God in his heart. He said that God's presence had to be maintained by the heart and by love rather than by understanding and speech.

"In the way of God," he said, "thoughts count for little, love does everything.""

"And it is not necessary," he continued, "to have great things to do. I turn my little omelette in the pan for the love of God; when it is finished, if I have nothing to do, I prostrate myself on the ground and adore my God, Who gave me the grace to make it, after which I arise, more content than a king. When I cannot do anything else, it is enough for me to have lifted a straw from the earth for the love of God.""

"People seek for methods of learning to love God. They hope to arrive at it by I know not how many different practices; they take much trouble to remain in the presence of God in a quantity of ways. Is it not much shorter and more direct to do everything for the love of God, to make use of all the labors of one's state in life to show Him that love, and to maintain His presence within us by this communion of our hearts with His? There is no finesse about it; one has only to do it generously and simply."

When one of the brothers persistently questioned Brother Lawrence about his means of practicing the presence of God, he answered with his usual simplicity:

"When I first entered the monastery, I looked upon God as the beginning and the end of all my thoughts and all the feelings of my soul. During the hours designated for prayer, I meditated on the truth and character of God that we must accept by the light of faith, rather than spending time in laborious meditations and readings. By meditation on Jesus Himself, I advanced in my knowledge of this lovable Person with Whom I resolved to dwell always.

"Completely immersed in my understanding of God's majesty, I used to shut myself up in the kitchen. There alone, after having done everything that was necessary for my work, I would devote myself to prayer in all the time that was left.

"The prayer time was really taken at both the beginning and the end of my work. At the beginning of my duties I would say to the Lord with confidence, 'My God, since You are with me, and since, by Your will, I must occupy myself with external things, please grant me the grace to remain with You, in Your presence. Work with me, so that my work might be the very best. Receive as an offering of love both my work and all my affections.'

"During my work, I would always continue to speak to the Lord as though He were right with me, offering Him my services and thanking Him for His assistance. And at the end of my work, I used to examine it carefully. If I found good in it, I thanked God. If I noticed faults, I asked His forgiveness without being discouraged, and then went on with my work, still dwelling in Him.

"Thus, continuing in this practice of conversing with God throughout each day, and quickly seeking His forgiveness when I fell or strayed, His presence has become as easy and natural to me now as it once was difficult to attain."

After he began to realize the great blessings this holy experience brings to the soul, Brother Lawrence advised all of his friends to practice it as carefully and faithfully as they could. Wanting them to undertake this act with a firm resolution and courage, he used the strongest reasons he could to persuade them. In his spiritual enthusiasm and by his godly example, he touched not only their minds, but penetrated their very hearts. He helped them to love and undertake this holy practice with as much fervor as they had previously regarded it with indifference. His example truly did serve better than his words. One had only to look at Brother Lawrence to desire to dwell in God's presence even as he did, no matter how rushed one might be.

Brother Lawrence called the practice of the presence of God the easiest and shortest way to attain Christian perfection and to be protected from sin.

Even when he was busiest in the kitchen, it was evident that the brother's spirit was dwelling in God. He often did the work that two usually did, but he was never seen to bustle. Rather, he gave each chore the time that it required, always preserving his modest and tranquil air, working neither slowly nor swiftly, dwelling in calmness of soul and unalterable peace.

In this intimate union with the Lord, our brother's passions grew so calm that he scarcely felt them any more. He developed a gentle disposition, complete honesty, and the most charitable heart in the world. His kind face, his gracious and affable air, his simple and modest manner immediately won him the esteem and the good will of everyone who saw him. The more familiar with him they became, the more they became aware of how profoundly upright and reverent he was.

Despite his simple and common life in the monastery, he did not pretend to be austere or melancholy, which only serves to rebuff people. On the contrary, he fraternized with everyone, and treated his brothers as friends, without trying to be distinguished from them. He never took the graces of God for granted, and never paraded his virtues in order to win esteem, trying rather to lead a hidden and unknown life. Though he was indeed a humble man, he never sought the glory of humility, but only its reality. He wanted no one but God to witness what he did, just as the only reward he expected was God Himself.

Although he was by nature reserved, he had no difficulty communicating his thoughts for the edification of his brothers. It was observed, however, that he favored those who were simpler and less sophisticated in their walk with Christ over the more enlightened. When he found such Christians, he shared everything he knew with them. With wonderful simplicity, Brother Lawrence disclosed to them the fairest secrets of the spiritual life and the treasures of divine wisdom. The sweetness that accompanied his words so inspired those who listened that they came away penetrated with the love of God, burning with the desire to put the great truths he had just taught them into practice.

Because God led Brother Lawrence more by love than by the fear of His judgment, his conversation tended to inspire the same kind of love. He encouraged other Christians to rely on God's love to lead them in their spirit-lives, rather than the knowledge of learned men. He used to tell his brothers, "It is the Creator Who teaches truth, Who in one moment instructs the heart of the humble and makes him understand more about the mysteries of our faith and even about Himself than if he had studied them for a long term of years."

It was for this reason that he carefully avoided answering those curious questions which lead nowhere, and which serve only to burden the spirit and dry up the heart. But when he was required by his superiors to declare his thoughts on the difficult questions that were proposed in conferences, his answers were always so clear and to the point that they needed no further comment. This remarkable ability was noticed by many learned men. An illustrious bishop of France, who had several interviews with him, said that God spoke directly to Brother Lawrence, revealing His divine mysteries to him because of the greatness and the purity of his love for Him.

Brother Lawrence loved to seek God in the things He had created. His soul, moved by the grandeur and the diversity of God's creations, became so powerfully attached to God that nothing could separate it from Him. He observed in each of creation's wonders God's wisdom, His goodness, and the different characteristics of His power. His spirit would become so filled at these times with admiration that he would cry out in love and joy, 'O Lord God, how incomprehensible art Thou in Thy thoughts, how profound in Thy designs, how powerful in all Thine actions."

Brother Lawrence's Christian walk began with this profound understanding of the power and the wisdom of God. This knowledge became the seed of all his perfection. In the beginning, faith was the only light he used to get to know God. As he matured, he would let nothing but faith guide him in all of God's ways. He often said everything he heard, everything he found written in books, and even everything that he himself wrote seemed pale in comparison to what faith revealed to him of the glory of God the Father and of Jesus Christ. In His own words:

"He alone is capable of making Himself known as He really is; we search in reasoning and in the sciences, as in a poor copy, for what we neglect to see in an excellent original. God Himself paints Himself in the depths of our soul. We must enliven our faith and elevate ourselves by means of that faith above all our feelings, to adore God the Father and Jesus Christ in all Their divine perfections, such as They are in Themselves. This way of faith is the mind of the Church, and it suffices to arrive at high perfection."

Brother Lawrence's principal virtue was his faith. As the just man lives by faith, so it was the life and nourishment of his soul. His spiritual life progressed visibly because of the way his faith quickened his soul. This great faith led him to God, elevating him above the world, which came to appear contemptible in his eyes. As a result, he sought happiness in God alone.

Faith was his greatest instructor. It was faith that gave him an unspeakably high esteem for Jesus Christ, the Son of God Who resides as King. He was so devoted to Jesus that he passed many hours, day and night, at His feet to render Him homage and adoration.

This same faith gave him a profound respect and love for the Word of God. Our brother believed that the books of even the most famous academies taught very little in comparison with God's great book. With such conviction did he believe the truth that faith taught him, that he often used to say that nothing he could read or hear in the world about God could satisfy him. Because God's perfection is infinite, He is consequently indescribable; no words are eloquent enough to give a complete description of His grandeur. 'It is only faith that makes me know Him as He is. By means of it I learn more about Him in a short time than I would learn in many years in the schools."

Faith gave Brother Lawrence a firm hope in God's goodness, confidence in His providence, and the ability to completely abandon himself into God's hands. He never worried about what would become of him; rather, he threw himself into the arms of infinite mercy. The more desperate things appeared to him, the more he hoped — like a rock beaten by the waves of the sea and yet settling itself more firmly in the midst of the tempest. This is why he said that the greatest glory one can give to God is to entirely mistrust one's own strength, relying completely on God's protection. This constitutes a sincere recognition of one's weakness and a true confession of the omnipotence of the Creator.

Brother Lawrence saw nothing but the plan of God in everything that happened to him. Because he loved the will of the Lord so much, he was able to bring his own will into total submission to it. This kept him in continuous peace. Even when told of some great evil in the world, He would simply raise his heart to God, trusting that He would work it to the good of the general order. Even when asked what he would answer if God gave him the choice of living or dying and going to heaven immediately, Brother Lawrence said that he would leave the choice to God, because he had nothing else to do but wait until God showed him His will.

The natural attachment to one's country that people carry with them into even the holiest places did not preoccupy him. He was equally loved by those who had opposite inclinations. He wished for good in general, without regard to the people by whom, or for whom, it was done. He was a citizen of heaven, not concerned with things on earth. His views were not limited by time, because he contemplated nothing but the Eternal One and had become eternal like Him.

The love of God reigned so completely in Brother Lawrence's heart that he turned all his affections toward this divine Beloved. Faith made him regard God as sovereign truth; hope made him think of Him as complete happiness; and love caused him to conceive of Him as the most perfect of all beings, as perfection itself.

Everything was the same to him — every place, every job. The good brother found God everywhere, as much while he was repairing shoes as while he was praying with the community. He was in no hurry to go on retreats, because he found the same God to love and adore in his ordinary work as in the depth of the desert.

Brother Lawrence's only means of going to God was to do everything for the love of Him. He was therefore indifferent about what he did. All that mattered was that he did it for God. It was He, and not the activity, that he considered. He knew that the more the thing he did was opposed to his natural inclination, the greater was the merit of his love in offering it to God. He knew that the pettiness of the deed would not diminish the worth of his offering, because God — needing nothing — considers in our works only the love that accompanies them.

Another characteristic of Brother Lawrence was an extraordinary firmness, which in another walk of life would have been called fearlessness. It revealed a magnanimous soul, elevated above the fear and the hope of all that was not God. He coveted nothing; nothing astonished him; he feared nothing. This stability of his soul came from the same source as all his other virtues. He had an exalted concept of God which made him think of Him as sovereign Justice and infinite Goodness. He was confident that God would not deceive him and that He would do him only good, because he was resolved never to displease Him and to do everything possible out of love for Him.

Far from loving God in return for His benefits, he would have loved Him even if there had been no punishment to avoid nor any reward to gain. He desired only the glory of God and the accomplishment of His holy will. This was especially evident in his final illness in which, even to his last breath, his spirit was so free that he expressed the same sentiments, as if he had been in perfect health.

The purity of his love was so great that he wished, if it were possible, that God could not see what he did in His service. This was so that he might act solely for God's glory and without self-interest. But God would let nothing pass without rewarding our brother a hundredfold, often causing him to feel delights and sensations of His divinity that were overwhelming. Then, he would cry out to God:

"It is too much, O Lord! It is too much for me.

"Give, if it please Thee, these kinds of favors and consolations to sinners and to the people who do not know Thee, in order to attract them to Thy service. As for me, who has the happiness of knowing Thee by faith, I think that must be sufficient. But because I ought not refuse anything from a hand so rich and generous as Thine, I accept, O my God, the favors Thou givest me. Yet grant, if it please Thee, that after having received them, I may return them just as Thou didst give them to me; for Thou knowest well that it is not Thy gifts that I seek and desire, but Thyself, and I can be content with nothing less."

Even these times of prayer would inflame his heart all the more with love, the effects of which he was not always able to contain. He was often seen, against his will, with his countenance quite radiant.

Regretting the early years before he dwelt in the love of God, Brother Lawrence would speak of this to his fellow-brothers:

"O Goodness, so ancient and so new, too late have I loved Thee!'"

"Do not act this way, my brothers. You are young; profit by the sincere confession I make to you of the little care I took to consecrate my first years to God. Consecrate all of yours to His love; for, as for me, if I had known sooner, and if anyone had told me, the things that I am telling you now, I would not have waited so long to love Him. Believe me, and count for lost all the time that is not spent in loving God."

Since loving God and loving one's neighbor are really the same thing, Brother Lawrence regarded those around him with the same affection he felt for the Lord. He believed that this was what Christ expressed in the Gospel: that anything he did for even the humblest of his brothers would be counted as being done for Jesus. He was particularly careful to serve his brothers no matter what he was doing, and especially when he was working in the kitchen. There he treated them as if they were angels, a charity that he inspired in all those who succeeded him.

He assisted the poor in their needs, as much as was in his power. He consoled them when they had problems, offering them his advice. To sum it up in a few words, he did all the good he could for his neighbor, and tried never to harm anyone. He did everything he possibly could to win men to God. Death did not frighten Brother Lawrence at all. On his deathbed, he displayed marks of a stability, a resignation, and a joy that were quite extraordinary. His hope became firmer and his love more ardent. If he had loved God deeply during his life, he did not love Him any less at death. But the virtue he esteemed above all others — faith — became particularly vigorous, penetrating him with its grandeur and enlightening him by its radiance.

He was given some final time alone to reflect on the great grace which God had given him during his life. When asked how he spent that time, he replied that he had been doing what he would be doing for all eternity—"Blessing God, praising God, adoring Him, and loving Him with all my heart. That is our whole purpose, brothers, to adore God and to love Him, without worrying about the rest."

The next day, February 12th, 1691, without any agony and without the loss of any of his senses, Brother Lawrence of the Resurrection died in the embrace of the Lord. At eighty years of age, he gave back his soul to God with the peace and tranquility of a person falling asleep. His death was like a gentle slumber which helped him pass from this life into a more blessed one. It is easy to conclude that his death was precious in the sight of the Lord, that it was very quickly followed by his reward, that he is now enjoying glory; and that his faith has been rewarded by clear vision, his hopes by possession, and his budding charity by a consummate love.

Printed in the United States
143536LV00003B/117/P